Marshall Sashkin, Ph.D.

Structured Activities
for Management Training
in Communication

**Organization Design
and Development, Inc.**
King of Prussia, Pennsylvania

Prepared for publication by Organization Design and Development, Inc., 2002 Renaissance Boulevard, Suite 100, King of Prussia, Pennsylvania, 19406. (215) 279-2002. Printed in the United States of America.

Library of Congress Catalog Card Number: 89-60508

ISBN: 0-925652-04-0

Permissions

"Frammus," "Nonverbal Communication," "Active Listening — Written Responses," "Active Listening — Verbal Responses," "Assessing Feedback Skills," "Developing Feedback Skills," "Trust — The President's Decision," "The Climate of Communication," and "The Johari Window," copyright 1984, in whole or in part, by Prentice-Hall, Inc. Adapted from Marshall Sashkin and William C. Morris, *Organizational Behavior: Concepts and Experiences.*

"The Garage Window" and "Asking Questions Right" copyright 1988 by Marshall Sashkin.

"Transparent Management" copyright 1987, Addison-Wesley Publishing Company. Adapted from Marshall Sashkin and William C. Morris, *Experiencing Management.*

"Bob, Carol, Ted and Alec" copyright 1978 by Organization Design and Development, Inc.

"Modern Manufacturing, Inc." copyright 1988 by Bradford Greason

Contents

Foreword

We are pleased to begin this series of structured learning activities with our first volume, *Structured Activities for Management Training in Communication*. What could be more useful than a well-tested collection of training activities in a subject we are all called upon frequently to facilitate? Our plans for future volumes will focus on the standard, but critical fare of leadership, motivation, and teamwork.

What makes these volumes unique is their orientation to the needs of trainers and program designers. We know, for example, when trainers receive a "design assignment" it usually goes something like this: "We have problems in _____ (you fill in the area). Can you help us out? Oh — and we need it yesterday."

Forget what you have heard about needs analysis, front-end analysis, or task analysis — this usually does not happen. Under time pressure to produce, trainers typically go to their files and pull out something they have done successfully before. Sure, they would like to try something new, but time and the need to be successful does not permit that luxury.

That is where a collection like this comes in handy. If you have a problem in leadership, communication, motivation, or teamwork (or any other subject or issue), you need to be able to put your hands on something right away that is guaranteed to work. That is the second aspect of this series that makes it different. The activities in this book have all been tried before — dozens, perhaps hundreds of times. And they will work for you, too.

Now for the last hurdle. Have you ever been "doing a session" and discovered that the directions were missing, incomplete, or just plain wrong? Panic sets in, followed by embarrassment and weakened self-esteem. With these activities we have given you all the directions we think you will need — so — you can't fail.

And who better to compile such a collection of activities? Marshall Sashkin, Associate Editor for the *HRD Quarterly*, is the former Associate Editor for the University Associates Annuals. During both of these assignments, Marshall has reviewed and edited hundreds of training activities. He has created many of his own and published these in several books. Marshall is among the most qualified designers of experiential materials in the United States. We take great pleasure in presenting the first volume in our series of management training activities.

Rollin Glaser
Organization Design and Development, Inc.

Using Structured Activities

This section has been prepared to assist trainers and program designers in using the structured activities in this book.[1] To do so, one must understand how structured activities fit into the experiential learning cycle.

The recommended learning model (Fig. 1) is based on the work of John Jones and David Kolb.[2] It has been expanded to include both training and learning activities, as well as some additional refinements. The program designer's pre-learning design activities include a performance needs analysis, the separation of training and development needs from other needs that may be contributing to performance problems, and a well-defined learning objective(s). It is assumed that these activities have been competently performed before the task of designing a learning module begins.

You will note that the learning cycle is framed with andragogical assumptions about adult learners and is situationally focused. Andragogical assumptions relate to the assumptions underlying the teaching/learning of adults. These assumptions, as identified by Malcolm Knowles, include the adult's tendency toward self-directedness; the use of the learner's experience in the learning process; the identification of learning needs based on work/life problems; and the adult's need to apply the learning to his/her immediate circumstances.[3] Whatever is done in the teaching/learning transaction takes into account those assumptions about adult learning needs.

In addition to the use of andragogical assumptions, a situational or contingency model should be incorporated into the learning strategy. Marshall Sashkin, Kenneth Blanchard, and Rollin Glaser have applied the situational leadership concept to trainer/teacher style.[4] Briefly, it is hypothesized that trainers will be most effective helping learners to acquire knowledge, attitudes, and skills if they adjust their style to the learner's developmental level.

Learners low in competence but committed to the learning project will probably respond to a more directive, informative style. Learners high in both competence and commitment may respond better to more self-directed strategies. A number of different developmental levels may be identified in our model. The point is that trainers can increase the probability that learning will occur in individuals or groups if they are sensitive to the developmental needs of the learners. "Situationally focused" means that the trainers, to the best of their ability, adjust their personal styles and learning strategies to match the developmental levels of their learners.

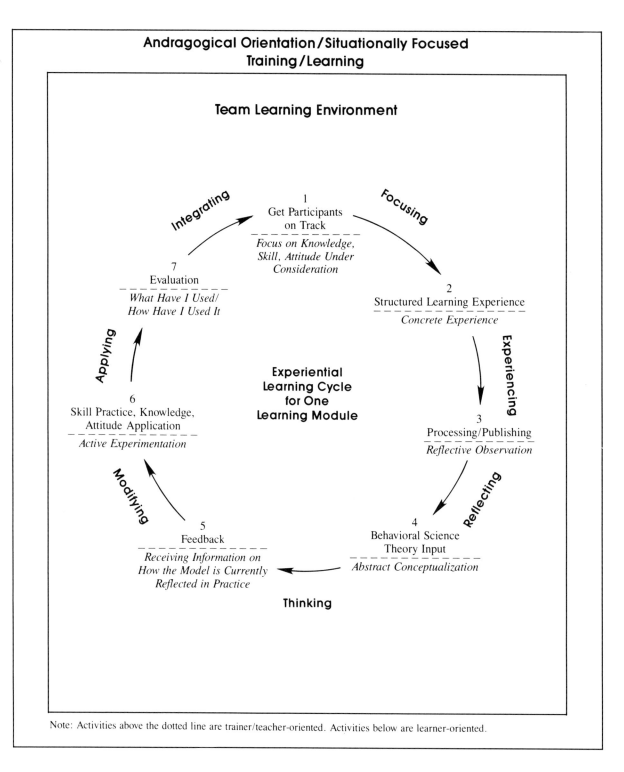

Fig. 1: Organization Design and Development
Training / Learning Model

Moving to the environment in which the learning cycle is embedded, you should note that a team learning format is suggested. People learn many things more effectively if they work in a small group of four to eight other learners. All of the processes in the experiential learning cycle — focusing, experiencing, reflecting, thinking, modifying, applying, and integrating — can be performed comfortably in a small group setting.

Many learning theorists conceive of the learning process as a cycle, meaning that if the steps are followed in sequence, a desired learning effect will be produced. Our learning model accepts the cycle notion, but increases the number of distinct steps from four to seven. This model further describes what trainers *and* learners are doing during each step in the cycle. By indicating both trainer and learner activities, program designers obtain a clearer picture of what needs to happen in each learning module. A learning module is defined as those training and learning activities that are conducted to reach a *single* learning objective.

The following describes the activities included in each of the seven steps in the learning cycle. To illustrate what might happen at each step, we will use the acquisition by a group of learners of a collaborative conflict resolution model as an example. Our purpose is to show how a program designer might use this cycle in preparing a learning module to help program participants learn how to think about and resolve conflict more effectively.

In Step 1, "Get Participants on Track," the trainer's problem is to help the participants relate to the concepts and skills about to be presented. The trainer wants to prepare the participants to attend to the learning objective. Participants need to "Focus on the knowledge, skill, or attitude under consideration." To accomplish this, the trainer might ask the participants to identify the connotations of the word "conflict."[5] The responses could be recorded and later analyzed for their implications regarding the subject. The trainer's expectation is that the participants will begin to attend to the knowledge, skill, or attitude under consideration and set themselves up for the learning to follow.

In Step 2, "Structured Learning Experience," the trainer introduces the participants to an activity that involves the group (or individuals) in a situation that is relevant to the concepts and skills being studied. The purpose of the structured learning experience is to provide the learners with a "Concrete Experience." Kolb defines a concrete experience as a ". . .here-and-now. . .experience to validate and test abstract concepts."[6] Structured experiences or activities come in a variety of formats: case studies, simulations, games, video/film vignettes, and many others. In our conflict example, the trainer might have the group engage in an exercise to have participants apply their present knowledge and skill to a variety of conflict situations. (See *Learning From Conflict*, "Round Robin: Rotating Chairs," pp. 177–178.[7]) The trainer creates several decks of conflict situation cards (3" x 5") known to be typical of this organizational setting. Participants sit around a rectangular table, one partner facing the other. A stack of conflict cards is available to each pair. Each pair takes one card from the stack and plays the roles required for three to five minutes. When time is called, each person assesses his/her success and his/her partner's success. Participants move one seat to the right, select a new card, and begin the process again with a new partner. The purpose of Step 2 then is to get participants to feel and react to a situation that is related to the concept or skill being presented. Both during and after the structured activity, the participants will probably have strong reactions related to their previous experiences with similar situations. These reactions provide the basis for the next step.

In Step 3, "Processing/Publishing," the participants are invited to reflect on and discuss their reactions to the structured activity. The purpose of the discussion is to get the participants to reflect critically on the activity and to process their reactions and similar past experiences. This discussion may be trainer or group directed. It may be public or private. Note that the learner's activity is referred to as "Reflective Observation." In terms of our conflict resolution example, participants would react to and discuss their feelings about each of the situations and their success or lack of it.

In Step 4, a "Behavioral Science Theory Input" is presented to clarify both the structured learning experience and the reflective observations of the participants. This input helps the learner by thinking. A behavioral science-based theory may be derived from a number of sources, preferably those that have a quantitative or qualitative basis. The delivery system for this theory could be the trainer giving a lecture (lecturette), showing a didactic film clip or video, or providing printed material. The participants may be asked to develop their own theories to explain Steps 2 and 3. Whatever the method selected, the purpose is to stimulate thought and enlighten minds. Generally, theory inputs incorporated into an experiential model are relatively short, ranging from five to twenty minutes. Relating this step to the conflict example, the trainer might describe Marshall Sashkin's five conflict styles as a way of conceptualizing people's typical responses to conflict situations.[8]

In Step 5, "Feedback," learners are provided with information about their current use of the knowledge, attitudes, or skills suggested by the theory. Kolb and others omit this as a formal step in the cycle. Yet, unless learners receive specific, objective information about their current performance as it relates to the theory, they may assume that they are already behaving in accordance with the model proposed. Learner feedback may be obtained in a variety of ways: learning instruments completed by the participants or others familiar with the participant, group feedback, feedback in pairs, or feedback from the trainer. The important event is the comparison learners make of their own behavior to the model. Is there a gap, and if so, how wide is it? Again, notice that the learner activity in Step 5 is "Receiving Information on How the Model is Currently Reflected in Practice." This step *may* lead to learners thinking about "modifying" their behavior to bring it more in line with theory. Connecting this step to our conflict example, the trainer might ask the participants to complete and score the *Conflict Style Inventory*.[9]

In Step 6, "Skill Practice, Knowledge, Attitude Application," learners are provided with an opportunity to practice and apply their new learning. The purpose of this step is to help learners incorporate these skills, knowledge, or attitudes into their personal repertoire by trying them out in a protected setting and considering how they might be used on the job or other life environment. This phase is referred to as "Active Experimentation." The learner tests the implications of newly acquired concepts in new situations. Step 6 may be handled in a variety of ways: critiqued role plays; solving work-related problems, performing work-related tasks; developing specific action plans that incorporate new knowledge, attitudes, or skills; or any one of a number of activities that cause the learner to try out the new learning. In our conflict illustration the participants may be asked to develop some typical conflict examples and roleplay these using their new concepts and skills.

Step 7, "Evaluation," requires a review of the learning effort, principally by the learner. The key questions to be answered are: "To what extent have I learned the new information, skills, or attitudes?" and "To what extent have I used the new knowledge, skills, or attitudes in the performance of my real-life roles?" The evaluation activity might be more accurately referred to as a process of *re-diagnosis*. "How has what I have learned affected my thinking and my behavior?" "What else do I need to learn or relearn?" Like the others, Step 7 might occur in a variety of ways: self-evaluation, colleague evaluation, supervisory review, predetermined performance measures, and other organizational indicators of change. In our conflict example, the learners might evaluate the number and quality of disagreements and conflicts with others following the learning experience.

Following Step 7 the cycle begins again. Notice that the arrows suggest movement and recycling. In summary, the terms on the arrows represent learning processes the learner is engaged in: focusing on what is to be learned; experiencing firsthand a representative problem; reflecting critically on similar problems and the feelings engendered; gaining a new perspective on a solution to the problem; receiving feedback on current practices; experimenting with new behaviors; transferring the new behaviors to the workplace or other life environment; and integrating the new knowledge, attitudes, and behaviors into the learner's personal thinking and acting.

Step	Description	Activity
Step 1	Get Participants on Track	Word Association
Step 2	Structured Learning Experience	Simulation, etc.
Step 3	Processing/Publishing	Group Discussion
Step 4	Behavioral Science Theory Input	Lecturette by Trainer
Step 5	Feedback	Inventory
Step 6	Skill Practice, Knowledge, Attitude Application	Role Play
Step 7	Evaluation	Supervisory Observation/ Feedback

Fig. 2: Applying the Model to Conflict Resolution Training

By following this seven-step model, the trainer and the learner are guided through a series of processes that will appeal to each of the learning styles likely to be found in a training/educational setting, thereby increasing the likelihood that learning will indeed occur. The job of the program designer becomes self-evident. Once the learning objectives have been established, materials to support the learning cycle must be found. That, of course, is the purpose of this collection of structured activities — to help the program designer/trainer fulfill Step 2 of the experiential learning model described above.

References

1. This section has been written by Rollin Glaser, president, Organization Design and Development, Inc.

2. David A. Kolb, *Experiential Learning*, Prentice-Hall, Englewood Cliffs, New Jersey, 1984. Annual Handbook for Group Facilitators, University Associates, La Jolla, California, 1972 to the present year.

3. M. S. Knowles, *The Modern Practice of Adult Education: From Pedagogy to Andragogy*, Second Edition, Cambridge Books, New York, 1980.

4. Paul Hersey and Ken Blanchard, *Management of Organizational Behavior: Utilizing Human Resources*, Fourth Edition, Prentice-Hall, Englewood Cliffs, New Jersey, 1982.

5. Lois B. Hart, *Learning From Conflict*, Organization Design and Development, Inc., King of Prussia, Pennsylvania, 1988, p. 31.

6. Kolb, *Op. Cit.*, p. 21.

7. Hart, *Op. Cit.*, pp. 177–178.

8. Marshall Sashkin, *Conflict Style Inventory*, Organization Design and Development, Inc., King of Prussia, Pennsylvania, 1986.

9. *Ibid.*

Structured Activity 1

The
Garage Window

Summary

This activity is intended as an icebreaker for use in communication training activities. It is a simple puzzle that very few people have ever encountered. It is extremely rare for anyone in a group to have the correct answer, which is a result of the necessary assumptions we make in order to simplify interpersonal communication. The activity makes the point well.

Contents

Trainer Instructions: Includes purpose, set-up, and step-by-step instructions for conducting the activity.

The Garage Window Problem: This problem sheet can be read to the group or copies can be handed out.

Solution Information: Gives the answer to the "Garage Window Problem" along with an explanation of the underlying lessons to be drawn. Not intended as a handout.

Trainer Instructions

Purpose

This activity is designed as an icebreaker for a training session on communication. It involves an uncommon puzzle or brainteaser that is exceptionally hard to solve because one must make a basic assumption about the definition of "window" that is slightly different from our normal assumption. Once that assumption is changed, however, the solution is obvious.

Set-Up

Any number of participants can be involved. The activity is best done with the entire group and not in small groups. Participants should be asked to think over the problem silently for a few minutes so that, in the unlikely event that someone knows (or figures out) the answer, the game will not be over too quickly. The entire activity takes about ten minutes.

Steps

1. Explain that as a kind of pretest to see how well participants can understand your communication, you are going to present a puzzle problem that actually has a simple and obvious solution. Ask that each person listen closely. Everyone should write down the answer before the group discusses the problem.

2. Read *The Garage Window Problem* (or hand out copies of the problem sheet).

3. Ask that everyone who has an answer write it down, drawing a picture of the garage window. Allow about five minutes.

4. Ask for volunteers to give their answers. Have some of the participants draw their solutions on a flip chart or chalkboard.

5. If someone has the correct answer, ask how that person figured it out. Make the point that this person, for some reason, had an image of a garage window that was different from the image most of us have. If no one has the answer, draw the correct answer on the flip chart or chalkboard and ask why no one figured it out.

6. Discuss with the group the concept of basic assumptions about the meaning of words and the definitions we share of many common terms. Ask whether they have experienced the kind of misunderstanding illustrated by the *Garage Window Problem* in other communication contexts. Try to get individuals to volunteer specific examples or give some of your own. Note that while we all share certain basic definitions as part of our common language, we also all differ in the implicit meanings we assign to similar or identical terms. When the differences are very small we may never even notice them, but when they are substantial they can lead to the same type of problem experienced in trying to solve the *Garage Window Problem* (except that the differences may never be uncovered).

The Garage Window Problem

This is a real problem. There are no tricks to it. Try your best to come up with a solution.

A man had a window in his garage door. He decided that this window was too small as it was only one foot high and one foot wide. To enlarge the window he used a saw to cut out the wood all around it. By doing so he was able to double the size of the window. But, to his surprise, when he measured it again it was still just one foot high and one foot wide. How can this be?

The Garage Window Problem
Solution

To most of us the word "window" means a square or rectangle with its top and bottom parallel to one another and to the horizon. However, a window can actually have any shape at all. The man's garage window was a perfect square, but it was installed with the corners pointing up and down, like a diamond. By sawing around it in a square so that it now looked like a "typical" window, with the top and bottom parallel to the ground and to one another, the actual area of the window is doubled. This can be proven geometrically. But the height and width dimensions remain the same — one foot. Once you see the pictures the solution is obvious.

The Garage Window Problem is, of course, a "set-up." Participants often will argue that if they had been told the truth they would have been able to solve the problem. But that is the point of the exercise: when we communicate with others we often act as though they know exactly what we mean, or at least that they use the same basic terms in the same manner. To some extent "meanings" are *always* in people and are not abstract truths that are firmly and clearly defined for all time. Just about any common term will not mean exactly the same thing to two different people. Only rarely is the difference so great as to be obvious, as in the case of the garage window.

Actually, languages are structured so as to minimize this problem; there is a lot of built-in redundancy. For example, if we were to leave out every fourth word on a page of non-technical text, we would generally be able to understand what was written without any great problem. But sometimes we depend too much on such hidden devices, and this can lead to some serious problems that are much more difficult to solve than the problem of the garage window.

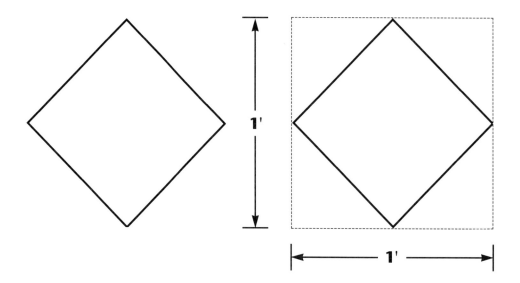

Structured Activity   2

Frammus

Summary

This activity demonstrates the value of two-way communication when giving instructions. The activity is based on a well-known exercise in which one person describes a figure composed of geometric shapes arranged in a certain pattern, and everyone listening tries to draw the figure without actually seeing it. The exercise is repeated allowing the participants to ask yes/no questions of the person who is describing the figure. Not surprisingly, the number of participants who draw the figure correctly is much higher when questions (two-way communication) are permitted. The present version is a more interesting and active variation using teams and involving role play.

Contents

Trainer Instructions: Contains purpose, details of the set-up, step-by-step instructions for conducting the activity, suggestions for variations, and discussion questions.

Background Information: Includes material to be read aloud to the group; need not be reproduced. A room layout is also provided.

Role for Syd Sharp: Instructions for the "communicator" role; includes a diagram showing the correct solution to the Frammus assembly problem.

Frammus Parts: The trainer must duplicate this sheet and cut out the pieces prior to the training session. The five Frammus pieces are to be placed in an envelope. Each person playing the role of Robin Earlie (the "receiver") is given an envelope with the five parts.

Trainer Instructions

Purpose

This activity is designed to demonstrate the importance of two-way communication, that is, communication that provides an opportunity for the receiver to check with the sender to determine whether the message was accurately received and understood. The activity is *not* designed to provide skill practice.

Set-Up

Any number of groups of three (triads) can participate. If there are two people left over they form a pair; one person left over joins a trio as a second messenger or may be assigned the role of observer. The activity usually takes at least one hour including discussion time.

A copy of the role for Syd Sharp (with the solution diagram) must be given to each person playing the role of Syd ("communicator"). The Frammus Parts sheet must also be copied, one per group, and the pieces cut out and put into an envelope. Each "receiver" (Robin) is given an envelope of pieces.

The activity works best using the room layout shown in the diagram, but any setting with moveable chairs can work as long as the receivers cannot see the solution diagram being viewed by one of the communicators in another group.

Steps

1. Explain to the group that the activity is about communication. Read the Background Information to the group.

2. Form groups of three. Two people, Syd and Robin, sit back-to-back, somewhat apart from each other. The third person (messenger) stands and acts like a teletypewriter, simply delivering Syd's message to Robin. Syd will whisper to the messenger who then whispers Syd's message to Robin.

3. Give each Syd a copy of his/her role information (with the solution diagram). Give each Robin an envelope containing the five Frammus pieces. The Syds read their roles while the Robins examine the Frammus pieces.

4. Explain that the aim is to assemble the Frammus correctly as quickly as possible. The first group to correctly assemble the Frammus is declared the winner, and a record will be kept of who is first, second, third, etc.

   [Note: The competition dynamic can be emphasized or de-emphasized depending on the desire of the trainer. For example, a prize might be provided for the fastest team. Alternatively, the trainer might decide not to mention the issue of competition.]

5. After about five minutes stop everyone and explain that Syd's teletypewriter has started working so that Syd can *receive* as well as *send* messages, meaning Robin can now ask questions.

6. After another five minutes stop everyone. If one group has solved the puzzle and correctly assembled the Frammus, make a note of the time and ask the three members of the winning team each to observe one of the groups not yet finished. Explain that Robin has become so frustrated as to actually pay a TV station to broadcast a picture of his/her attempt to assemble the Frammus, so Syd can watch and give better instructions — still using the teletypewriter. Syd now stands in front of Robin so as to "watch" what Robin is doing, while continuing to communicate through the messenger. Remind Syd that Robin is still not to be shown the solution diagram. Allow fifteen minutes or until most groups succeed in assembling the Frammus.

7. Announce the "winners" (if the competition aspect has been included). Bring the group back together for a discussion of the principles involved in and demonstrated by this activity.

Variation

This activity is based on a classic exercise on one-way/two-way communication first developed by Harold Leavitt and Fritz Mueller in 1951. If the trainer wishes, the activity can be done in the original manner by having one person instruct the entire group in how to assemble the Frammus. Everyone will then need a set of Frammus parts. The volunteer is given the diagram of the assembled Frammus and standing so that the others cannot see him or her (or with back to the group) tries to explain how to assemble the Frammus. No questions are allowed. After about five minutes, the trainer checks to see if anyone has successfully assembled the Frammus parts. (This is not likely.) The volunteer then continues to instruct the group, this time in full view of the group. (This permits nonverbal cues between the volunteer and the group members and generally results in several correct solutions.) Finally, the volunteer continues giving directions and is allowed to respond to "yes" or "no" questions from the group. This generally leads most group members to solve the problem within a few minutes.

Invariably, participants experience the "zero feedback" (out of sight) situation as extremely difficult, if not impossible. The very limited feedback situation in which the participants can see the volunteer but cannot ask questions is also quite difficult. It is possible, however, that a few people will succeed in assembling the Frammus. The feedback condition, with yes/no questions allowed, generally results in many successful solutions. The point is to show that direct, simple feedback is important for accurate communication.

Discussion Questions

1. Did any group succeed in the first "round" when only the one-way teletypewriter was available? Why (or why not)?

2. What proportion of the groups succeeded when two-way communication was available? Why was it that all of the groups did not succeed?

3. What were the important factors for success under visual feedback conditions? Try to identify relevant structural and process factors.

Background Information

Syd Sharp is a successful inventor. Syd's latest creation is an automated problem indicator called a "Frammus." Syd has offered the Frammus to Robin Earlie, President of Earlie-Byrd Manufacturing Company. Unfortunately, the sample Frammus that Syd sent for examination was damaged in the mail. The pieces arrived in an envelope with a note from the postmaster expressing sincere regrets. Robin tried to reassemble the Frammus, after noting that none of the parts was damaged, but couldn't seem to get it right. On trying to reach Syd by phone, Robin found that Syd was on vacation in a remote area. A messenger was dispatched, and the messenger succeeded in finding Syd and explaining the problem. Syd was able to locate a telex — a teletypewriter — but the machine could only send, not receive, messages. Nonetheless, Syd tried to explain to Robin how to assemble the Frammus.

Room Layout

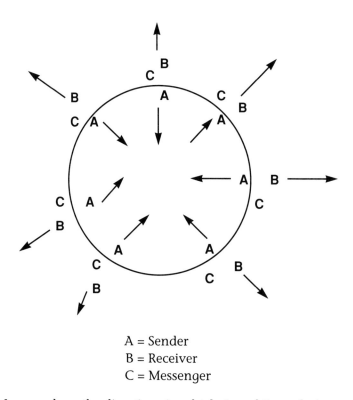

A = Sender
B = Receiver
C = Messenger

Arrows show the directions in which A and B are facing

Role For Syd Sharp

Your new Frammus is an automated problem indicator. A complex electro-magnetic timer operates a mechanism that pulls together five oddly shaped pieces that are connected by threads. The pieces meet to form a perfect "F," short for "foul-up." The Frammus you sent to Robin Earlie consisted only of the five parts, excluding the timer and thread assembly, and was intended for demonstration only. You are to instruct Robin, through the telex, so Robin can assemble the Frammus. The diagram below shows the five pieces and how they fit together to form the Frammus.

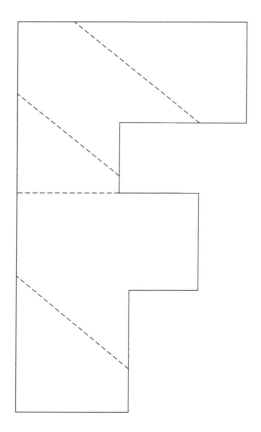

Frammus Parts

Directions: These parts are to be cut out. When properly assembled they form a perfect Frammus. Each "Robin" should receive an envelope of the pieces.

Structured Activity   3

Nonverbal Communication

Summary

The purpose of this activity is, first, to illustrate common nonverbal signals that we all use but rarely attend to explicitly and, second, to explore the power of nonverbal, as compared with verbal, communication. Most nonverbal messages deal with feelings that, though they may be hidden, are often far more potent than the rational parts of the message. This is a simple activity with a potentially powerful learning impact.

Contents

Trainer Instructions: Contains purpose, details of the set-up, step-by-step instructions for conducting the activity, and discussion questions. No further materials are needed except for paper and pencils.

Trainer Instructions

Purpose

The aim of this exercise is to illustrate common nonverbal signals and to explore the potency or power of nonverbal communication as compared to verbal communication. Most nonverbal communication deals with feelings and, though they may be hidden, feelings are typically much more powerful than the rational parts of messages — the "facts."

Set-Up

Any number of participants can take part in this activity in small groups of three to five people. There is no specific requirement that all groups be of a particular size and groups may even be of different sizes. The activity takes from thirty minutes to an hour depending on how much discussion time is allowed. The only materials needed are paper and pencils for the participants.

Steps

1. Form small groups of three, four, or five people. Neither the number of groups nor the number in a group is especially important, but each group should have at least three people; five per group is about right.

2. Ask each participant to write down privately three specific feelings (e.g., happy, sad, irritated). Ask that at least one of the terms selected be different from the type of examples suggested.

3. Each of the group members is to try to communicate nonverbally one of the feelings he/she wrote down, without showing anyone the list. After a minute or so of trying to communicate the feeling, the other group members try to guess what it was. The person who was trying to communicate then tells the group what the feeling really was and records how many were correct. Each member of the small group takes a turn, using a feeling different from any that were used previously. (If there is time, participants can be asked to go around the group a second time.)

4. Bring the entire group back together to review the results. Look at how accurate participants were in general. Discuss the issue of accuracy of nonverbal communication with the entire group.

5. Return to the small groups. Repeat Step 3, except that while a group member is giving a nonverbal message, he/she is to give, at the same time, a *different* verbal message. The verbal message need not be opposite to the nonverbal message, just different. For example, smile (nonverbal) at the same time you are saying, "I find this kind of behavior very upsetting."

6. Bring the group together again for a final discussion. Examine the differences between the two efforts. Did the different verbal message make it harder to pick up on the nonverbal message? Consider some of the following questions:

Discussion Questions

1. How accurately were participants able to understand the first round of non-verbal messages? Were more subtle or less common feelings harder to identify?

2. What happened to the level of accuracy when a different verbal signal was present?

3. When different verbal and nonverbal messages are being communicated in a real situation, which are people more likely to "hear" and concentrate on? Why?

Structured Activity   4

Active Listening:
Written Responses

Summary

This activity provides the minimum basic introduction required for sound development of the active listening skill. Active or "empathetic" listening is a basic and critical communication skill. Restating what another person says, including the other's feelings, may sound simple. Even though most people can learn this skill it does take more time and practice than one might expect. A full-blown workshop would normally take a day; a solid, skill-building introductory session should last four hours; a basic introduction can be accomplished in as little as one hour. In this activity a set of ten items is read to the participants who identify the feeling being expressed and write a very brief restatement of what was said, using their own words and showing an understanding of the feeling expressed. Individual participants are called on to give sample restatements, with some group discussion, before going on to the next item. A worksheet is provided for this activity.

Contents

Trainer Instructions: Contains purpose, details of the set-up, step-by-step instructions for conducting the activity, and discussion questions.

Active Listening: Written Responses: A copy of this fill-in form should be given to each participant.

Trainer Instructions

Purpose

This activity is designed as the first step in learning the skill of "active listening," that is, demonstrating understanding by restating in one's own words the content and affect (feelings) expressed by another person. Obviously, active listening is a verbal, not a written, skill. However, by using written rather than verbal responses, participants can go slowly and revise their initial attempts. It is important to deal with one statement fully before going on to the next one. That way participants build on what they have learned throughout the activity.

Set-Up

Any number of people can participate in this activity, but, to allow for the greatest involvement of the participants, the practical limit in group size is about thirty. The entire activity can be completed in forty-five minutes. This time can be reduced by skipping a few of the statements on the Active Listening: Written Responses form. Each participant will need a copy of this form and a pen or pencil. Desks or something to write on will be helpful; the exact room arrangement is not important.

Steps

1. Define "active listening" for the group. If possible demonstrate active listening with one of the participants. Explain that the aim of this activity is to begin to build active listening skills.

2. Pass out copies of the Active Listening: Written Responses form. Explain that each of the ten statements is a comment made by an employee to his or her boss. The entire group will work on one statement at a time. Each person will imagine he/she is the boss and will compose a response that restates, in his/her own words, what the employee said, as well as identifying the employee's feelings.

3. Begin with the first statement. Read the statement to the group as though you were the employee. Ask participants to identify the employee's feelings by writing in the box labelled "Feeling" the way they think the employee felt when he/she made the statement. Repeat the statement a few times to give participants a chance to listen for the feeling. Then ask what the feeling was; ask for volunteers or call on individuals to state the feeling they identified. Get several responses. Try to get the group to agree on the feeling that was expressed. Suggest that they avoid general categories like "upset" or "frustrated" and try instead to identify a clear, specific feeling like "angry," "annoyed," or "irritated."

4. Now ask each person to write in the space provided on the form a restatement of what the employee said, using different words as though the participant were speaking to the employee directly. The restatement must also include acknowledgement of the employee's feelings.

5. After about three minutes ask for volunteers to read their restatements to the group. If necessary call on a few individuals. Discuss which responses seem to get at the content and the feeling best.

6. Repeat the above steps for each of the ten statements on the Active Listening: Written Responses form. You may need to read the statements "dramatically" to emphasize and make sure everyone hears the underlying feelings. By the tenth statement every-one should be writing accurate responses with little difficulty.

Discussion Questions

1. Are some feelings harder to identify than others? Why? Are some feelings more difficult to express in a restatement? Why?

2. What happens if you are trying to restate what another person said and felt, but you guess the wrong feeling? What are the consequences?

3. Is there a "best" restatement for every statement?

Active Listening: Written Responses

Statement	Feeling	Restatement
1. John is really getting to me because of the way he insists on doing the Tomkins' job *his* way.		
2. I'll either do it or have it done on time — you can count on it!		
3. If you didn't keep giving us these unexpected rush jobs, there wouldn't be so many errors!		
4. I really thought the report was so good it would get top management's praise, let alone approval. Now, it seems that they just don't care.		
5. Why don't you get off my back!		
6. What's this about me being scheduled for overtime on Saturday? I worked *last* Saturday and it's not my turn this week!		
7. I read over your procedural proposal. We tried a procedure like that two years ago; it didn't work then and I don't know why it would now.		
8. I can think of better ways to spend my time than in these pointless, endless meetings!		
9. Can you tell me about this appraisal session coming up? Will all the problems of the past year be reviewed?		
10. You shouldn't bawl me out in front of everyone! What will they think?		

Structured Activity   5

Active Listening:
Verbal Responses

Summary

This activity introduces a second aspect of the active listening skill and should immediately follow Structured Activity 4. The activity begins with the entire group continuing active listening practice, now giving a direct verbal response to the trainer rather than writing down a response. After a few practice rounds groups of three are formed. One person reads an item, the second tries to give an accurate restatement (in his or her own words) that shows understanding of the feeling and the content message, and the third person listens and then critiques the second person. Each person has the opportunity to try all three roles. Ten statements are provided on a sheet.

Contents

Trainer Instructions: Contains purpose, details of the set-up, step-by-step instructions for conducting the activity, a variation, and discussion questions.

Active Listening: Verbal Responses: A copy of this form is needed for each participant.

Active Listening: This is a summary handout describing active listening.

Trainer Instructions

Purpose

A generally recognized skill that facilitates effective communication has various names: empathic listening, listening for feelings, and paraphrasing are some common labels for the skill we call "active listening." This skill requires the listener to restate in his/her own words what he/she heard the speaker say and to include in the restatement an identification of the feeling expressed by the speaker. Active listening has been widely used since it was first identified by Carl Rogers in the 1940's. In this activity participants build on the written paraphrasing skill developed in the previous structured activity by practicing verbal restatement responses. The activity is set up so that everyone has an opportunity to practice and receive feedback on their efforts.

Set-Up

Any number of people can participate. Ideally, the total should be divisible by three in order to form small groups for the second part of the activity. If necessary one group can be a pair; if there is a single person "left over" form two pairs by splitting up one group of three. This activity is greatly facilitated by a large room with moveable chairs.

The activity usually takes at least an hour and can easily take two hours. More time will be needed if Structured Activity 4 (Active Listening: Written Responses) has not been carried out prior to this activity.

While it is strongly recommended that the previous activity, "Active Listening: Written Responses," be used first, it is possible to use the "Verbal Responses" activity without having first used the other. In that case the trainer should plan to spend substantially more time at the start of the activity in working with the entire group on practice examples. Instead of using only the first three or four items on the "Active Listening: Verbal Responses" form, the trainer can use items from the "Active Listening: Written Responses" form as well.

Each participant must have a copy of the "Active Listening: Verbal Responses" form. This form is used by the entire group to follow along during the first part of the activity and is also used by the groups of three. For the small groups, the top half of the form gives the statement for one person to read to a second person who is to make the active listening response. The bottom half of the form is used by the third person who observes and rates the effectiveness of the active listening response.

Steps

1. If Structured Activity 4 has been used, explain that the present activity is an extension of one they have already experienced. Instead of writing their responses, as in Structured Activity 4, participants will make responses orally as would be done in a real situation.

2. Give each participant a copy of the "Active Listening: Verbal Responses" form. The trainer reads aloud the first statement (trying to express the feelings implied by the statement) as though speaking directly to the person identified on the form (a friend, in the case of the first statement).

3. Ask participants to identify the feeling expressed. If there are few or no volunteers, call on specific individuals. Try to get clarity on the underlying nature of the feeling. In the case of the first statement, the feeling the trainer should try to express is disappointment. It is not necessary that there be complete agreement on the precise feeling, but responses that are far off target should be explored (e.g., "Why do you think the feeling was anger?" "What would the statement have sounded like if anger were being expressed?").

4. The trainer reads the statement again and then asks for active listening responses. Explain that the response must include an identification of the feeling expressed. Again, if there are few volunteers call on specific individuals. Get several responses to show that a variety of "correct" responses is possible; that there are *many* accurate ways to make an active listening response to the *same* statement.

5. Repeat the above steps using the first three or four items on the "Active Listening: Verbal Responses" form. Make sure that every participant either volunteers or is called on to respond. If the group is relatively small, start on one side of the room and work over to the other side, person by person.

6. Hold a brief discussion to talk over what individuals did correctly or incorrectly. Also discuss the nature of the active listening skill and make sure that everyone accurately understands what it is and how it is done (even though many will not yet be adept at using the skill).

7. Form groups of three. If there is a single group of two, this group participates as a team (the trainer may wish to observe them occasionally and offer some feedback). If a single person is "left over" a team of three should be split up to form two pairs.

8. Each small group works on the remaining items on the "Active Listening: Verbal Responses" form. Each person gets two turns as speaker, as listener, and as an observer. Thus, one person reads an item while the person who is listener responds with an active listening restatement of what the speaker said, using the listener's own words, including a statement of the feeling the listener believes the speaker tried to communicate. The third group member observes and critiques the listener's response using the "Active Listening: Verbalization" part of the form. After two tries the group members switch roles and go on to the next two items with a new speaker, listener, and observer. The above process is repeated and when completed they switch again for a third and final round. Each participant has a chance to take on all three roles and has two specific tries at using the active listening skill and getting feedback from a peer.

9. The group members reassemble for a general discussion of what they have experienced and learned.

Variation

If this activity is accomplished fairly quickly or works especially well, you may wish to continue the activity on an "ad lib" basis. A simple way to do this is to continue with small groups of three. Each person identifies a problem situation (preferably not one that is of great or immediate importance) and writes down a few notes about the situation. One of the triad members tries to explain his/her problem to a second person while the third person observes. The second person tries to use the active listening skill to explore the first person's problem for about three minutes. The observer then critiques the second person's active listening behavior. This action is repeated twice so that each person has a chance to practice the active listening skill. The entire group can then discuss how it felt to try active listening in a more realistic situation as well as the difficulties in using active listening in a real situation.

Discussion Questions

1. Did listeners who tried active listening later in the activity find it easier than those who went first?

2. Did individual group members find active listening to be easier on their second attempt? Did practice seem to help?

3. When would active listening be especially useful? When might it not be very helpful?

4. In what real-life situations might participants try out active listening? Are there any low- or no-risk situations that could be used to practice active listening?

Active Listening: Verbal Responses

Interaction	Statement
Friends	1. I went through a lot to get my degree and become an architect, but after two years I really don't enjoy the work.
Friends	2. It's a great opportunity, but it's so risky!
Co-workers	3. Ever since he got that promotion he's been a stranger to me, as though he's too good to have anything to do with old friends.
Friends	4. I'm determined to make a go of it with this business! No matter what, I'll stick it out and see it through.
Subordinate to Boss	5. I can't help it! I've been patient, but I'm just so sick and tired of doing all the work on that project! If Joe can't do his share, I can't do it for him!
Subordinate to Boss	6. You know, I do make my share of mistakes, but I don't see why I should be blamed for *everything* that goes on around here!
Co-workers	7. He took credit for that report and used it to get the merit raise I deserved, but *I'll* show *him*!
Friends	8. Getting to the top is what counts — it's what drives me. I'm bound to get there, too, no matter who I have to step over!
Friends	9. I trusted them, and they took me for a real ride!
Co-workers	10. I feel sorry for Fred — I know he's had more than his share of trouble — but I have to get my own responsibilities taken care of first. Then, if I can, I'll see what I can do for him.

Active Listening: Verbalization

1. Feeling, As You Identify It	Feeling, As Active Listener Stated It

2. Overall, how accurate was the active listener in paraphrasing?

Completely	Mostly	Partly	Not At All
☐	☐	☐	☐

Examples:

Active Listening

Listening is usually considered a passive state in which you are the "receptacle" of information and your job is merely to try to concentrate on the message and understand it. Actually, effective listening is active, not passive, and requires skill and practice. To understand and learn effective listening skills, we must break them down into their smallest components.

The first "chunk" of listening skill is called *attending*. This consists of postural, visual, and nonverbal indicators that show you are really paying attention to the other person. Three specific behavioral skill elements are characteristic of attending. First is physical body *posture*, such as leaning forward in an open, accepting, neutral position (such as arms *un*crossed). When sitting "bolt upright" in a chair, legs and arms crossed, one displays the exact opposite of attending. The second behavioral element involves *eye contact*. When you look away from the person who is talking, you are not displaying attending behavior. This does not mean you should "stare down" the other person, just that you must regularly let your eyes make contact. Finally, some vocal (but nonverbal) expressions *encourage* the other person to keep talking — things like a nod of your head, a smile, or saying, "Um-hmm." These expressions show the other person that you want to hear more. We all know how to be attentive, but we are often lazy or sloppy about doing so. It is helpful to remind yourself to apply attending skills and even to practice them occasionally.

The second group of skill elements can be called *active listening*, which is much less common than attending. Active listening includes three subskills. The first, simple *repetition*, is used only to clarify what you did not hear — the signal — or are not sure you heard correctly. This is as far as most people go with listening skill, and it is not adequate. The second element involves *paraphrasing*, or repeating in your own words what the other person said. This lets you determine whether or not you correctly interpreted the meaning of what the other person said.

Correct paraphrasing requires more active involvement in the listening process than simple repetition, but it is a skill that is relatively easy to learn. The third and most difficult skill element is *listening for feelings* and restating the feeling that the other person has expressed. This skill is difficult to develop for two reasons: first, you must restate the other person's feelings in your own words, not just repeat the term the other person used; and second, you must often figure out just what the other person's feeling is. Sometimes this is obvious, as it is, for example, when someone is very angry and yelling or is very sad and crying. Often, however, our feelings are more subtle and less overt parts of the message. Moreover, you must figure out how to restate the feeling without appearing to be negative or hostile, and this may take some tact. The other person might become very offended if you said, "You seem to feel very jealous of Paul now that he got the promotion and you didn't." If you are accurate, the other person might be even more offended! A better way to state this person's feeling would be, "You feel pretty disappointed at losing that promotion to Paul." This would be better, even if it is a little less accurate than had you labelled the feeling as envy or jealousy.

Paraphrasing combined with listening for feelings is at the heart of active listening. This is the only way to make certain that one person has correctly understood what another person meant. Consider: John says, "The Greenway project is *way* overdue!" What does he mean? Does he mean, "We're in trouble and I'm upset!"? Does he mean, "The project leader is in for trouble!"? Or does he mean, "Our schedule is all fouled up and that upsets me!"? To find out, you might say, "You feel concerned that we are so far off our scheduled project deadlines." Or, you might say, "You seem distressed that we haven't gotten out Greenway on time." These or a wide range of other active listening responses would be equally effective; all serve the same purpose: letting the other person know what you heard and checking for accuracy. John might respond, "Right!" Or, he might say, "No, it's not the overall schedule, it's this client who will probably raise hell with division management!" In one sense it does not really matter, because whatever John's response is, you will now know for certain what he really meant.

Of course, your response could have been, "What do you mean by that, John?" John might then respond with a clarification — but his clarification might still leave *you* in the dark! How often has that happened to you? Alternatively, John might say, "Didn't I just *say* that we're way overdue?" By rephrasing the content and feeling stated in John's message, you show that you are trying to listen for understanding, that you are willing to go halfway with the other person to try to really hear what was said. That is why this is called active listening, because the listener becomes an active participant in the communication process instead of assuming the typical passive role.

A conversation composed only of active listening responses would be very dull. In fact, it would probably be hard to keep such a conversation going for very long, because the parties would quickly begin to repeat what each other had said and felt over and over again. Active listening is useful for specific purposes, not for general conversation. The major purpose is to provide a special kind of feedback, so that the sender knows for sure that the message was heard correctly. Another reason for using active listening is to get the other person to "open up" so that a problem or issue can be explored in depth. People are more likely to be open when they see that you are trying actively to understand them without being a judge. Still another use for active listening is to let the other person hear and think over what he is really saying. Sometimes we are surprised by our own comments when we actually listen to what we said!

The logical follow-up to active listening would be questions, comments, or feedback. Active listening facilitates the communication process, but it is not itself a *model* of this process.

Structured Activity 6

Asking
Questions
Right

Summary

This activity aims at teaching participants experientially the difference between open and closed-end questions. The aim is to give participants a broader range of questioning skills by demonstrating how to phrase and use questions that are partly open, completely open, and completely closed. The activity starts with a conceptual introduction (a lecturette) by the trainer followed by practice in the large training group. When the activity has been modeled a few times, groups of three are formed, and participants are given the opportunity to practice and receive feedback within their triad. A set of questions to be restated (as open, closed, or in-between) is provided along with sample restatements. A brief, one-page handout is included.

Contents

Trainer Instructions: Contains purpose, details of the set-up, step-by-step instructions for conducting the activity, and discussion questions

Asking Questions: This form is to be used by the trainer and later in groups of three for individual practice and critique. One copy is needed for each participant.

Sample Restatements: Contains examples of ways to restate questions so as to make closed questions more open and excessively open questions more limited and focused. Can be given to each participant if desired following the practice session.

Asking Questions: This is a brief handout for participants.

Trainer Instructions

Purpose

This activity is aimed at developing skill in phrasing questions that facilitate the communication process. Most people ask questions that are either too broad and unfocused ("So, what's new with you?") or too narrow and limiting ("Did you like the play?"). In the first example communication is not helped along because the other person really has no "hook," nothing to hang on to as a focus for a response. Thus, the typical response is quite vague and noncommittal ("Oh, not much"). The second example is "closed" because the only logical answers are "Yes," "No," "Somewhat," and "I'm not sure." Unless the other person takes the initiative the conversation ends. To open up the conversation one must use focused and open questions. A focused question might be, "Have you gone to any new shows lately?" To phrase it as an open question you could say, "What did you think of the play?" This activity begins with the instructor explaining the nature of open and closed questions and then using the first few items on the "Asking Questions" form to elicit and shape responses from participants. The skills are practiced individually in small groups using the remaining questions on the form. Note that this activity does not attempt to make participants into highly skilled interviewers; it is aimed at improving normal, conversational questioning skills.

Set-Up

Any number of people can participate. After the trainer's initial presentation groups of three are formed. If necessary, there may be a group of two. If there is just one person left over, he/she should be an observer. The activity usually takes forty minutes to an hour depending on the length and depth of the discussion after the practice.

A copy of the "Asking Questions" form will be needed for each participant. The activity is much easier to conduct in a room with moveable chairs, but any room is useable.

Steps

1. The trainer gives a brief lecturette on asking questions, defining and illustrating open, focused, and closed questions. (See the handout for examples and a basic overview.)

2. Using the first three or four questions on the "Asking Questions" form, the trainer asks the participants to try restating the questions to make them moderately open and focused. (Note that several participants can be asked to respond to the same question, giving alternative restatements.)

3. Form groups of three. Hand out copies of the "Asking Questions" form. Each triad is to select one person to begin as questioner. The questioner restates the first question on the form, not already used by the trainer. The other group members critique. The questioner tries again, using the next question on the form. Again the others critique the restatement. Then the next group member becomes the questioner, using the next two questions on the form. When he/she is finished the third group member has a turn with the final questions on the form. Allow about fifteen to twenty minutes for this group practice. (Note: Each questioner can first write his/her restatements on the handout form if desired.)

4. Bring the entire group back together for a final discussion.

Discussion Questions

1. Did the last person to practice find it easier than the first person? Was he/she more accurate in making the questions on the form more focused?

2. Are completely open questions ever appropriate and useful? When? Why? Are completely closed questions ever appropriate and useful? When? Why?

3. What additional questioning skills are needed if one is to be a good interviewer?

Asking Questions

Question	Restatement
1. Tell me something about yourself?	1.
2. Do you like your job?	2.
3. How do you feel about your work?	3.
4. Is your boss a good supervisor?	4.
5. What is this company like?	5.
6. Are you planning to quit?	6.
7. What do you do at work?	7.
8. Can you take a day off if you want to?	8.
9. How is your department set up?	9.
10. Is your pay adequate?	10.

Sample Restatements

1. Where are you from?
   What kind of work do you do?

2. What are the three things you like best about your job?
   What would you change about your job if you could?

3. How satisfied are you with your present job?
   What is your present level of job satisfaction?

4. What are some examples of how your boss gives directions or assignments?
   How do people at your level rate your boss' managerial skills?

5. How formal are things in this company?
   How much concern for employees does this firm seem to have?

6. What job alternatives, if any, have you recently considered?
   What could happen to make you want to quit this job?

7. What are your three most important job duties?
   What are some examples of what you might do in a typical morning?

8. What sort of vacation and leave policies does your firm have?
   How often do you take a day off just because you feel like it?

9. How many different job positions or offices are there in your department?
   What is the chain of reporting responsibility within your own department?

10. How satisfied are you with your current pay?
    How well does this firm pay compared with similar companies in the area?

Asking Questions

While we all know how to ask questions, few of us are really skilled in asking questions that help the communication process. Such effective questioning can be extremely helpful to a manager in his or her daily work interactions. Of course, in formal interviews, asking questions is more than a skill—it can become an art. But for most purposes it is quite enough to be able to understand the different "levels" of questions, from completely open to completely closed, and to be able to ask a question at whatever level seems appropriate to the context and circumstances.

Far too many questions are of the completely closed variety: "Do you like chocolate ice cream?" Such questions permit only four possible responses: "Yes," "No," "Somewhat," and "I don't know." In other words, we do not generally use the entire range of question types available nor do we stop to decide what type of a question is appropriate for a given situation.

At the opposite extreme is the completely open question: "What's new with you?" or "What do you think?" This is probably the second most common type of question. Very often it imposes too little structure on the other person's response and is not much better for gaining information than the overstructured, completely closed question.

There are, however, several intermediate levels of questions that are usually much more helpful than those at the extremes. This is because intermediate-level questions focus the other person's response without limiting it so much that important information is lost. The simplest way to limit an open question is to be specific about the particular topic or issue: "Tell me about the quality of communication in this company." The response can be focused even more by narrowing the question a bit further: "Give me a couple of examples of good and poor communication that you personally recall, things that you have observed over the past few weeks." You can become still more focused by further defining the topic: "Can you give me some examples that deal with supervisor-employee communication?" Even if you just want a general categorical answer to a question, there is no need to limit yourself to just two categories (yes or no). That is, you can ask for an answer that refers to a finer set of categories: "Regarding the quality of communication in this company, if a "1" were to represent completely ineffective communication and a "5" were perfect communication, how would you rate communication in this company?"

Now, however, we are approaching the formal data collection interview and we will not examine such formal interview situations here. However, one useful skill that comes out of the art of interviewing is "probing." The probe is a special type of question. Probes are short open questions, gestures, or even silences that indicate an interest in digging deeper into a particular topic or issue. Examples would be a "quizzical" facial expression (eyebrows raised and eyes wide open), or a brief question like, "Then what?" or "How did you deal with that?" Sometimes the best probe is silence. All too often we talk just to fill an uncomfortable silence. It is usually helpful to just wait for the other person to speak, to "pause and probe," even if this feels strange. The other person will generally feel just as uncomfortable with the silence. By waiting for the other person to speak first you will get more information than if you just asked another question. Sometimes a pause-probe will elicit information that a person would not give in response to a direct question.

Learning to ask effective questions is not really difficult, but it does take thought and, like any skill, practice. The result will be an increase in the quality of the information you get and that information is more likely to meet your needs than is the information you would get from either the yes-no or the completely open type of question.

Structured Activity 7

Assessing
Feedback Skills

Summary

A very brief (six-item) questionnaire is used to provide a self-assessment of feedback skills. Each item on the questionnaire is tied directly to one of a set of six guidelines or "rules" for giving effective feedback. These six rules were derived from a variety of classic sources on effective feedback, and other similar versions are commonly used in communication skills training. The questionnaire helps to focus participants on their own skills and provides the trainer with a good opportunity for a brief lecturette that participants will find interesting because it relates to their own questionnaire results.

Contents

Trainer Instructions: Contains purpose, details of the set-up, step-by-step instructions for conducting the activity, and discussion questions.

Feedback Skills Questionnaire: A copy of this brief, one-page questionnaire is needed for each participant.

FSQ Scoring Norms: Gives distribution and norms for the FSQ which can be used as a master for an overhead. The information can be put on a chalkboard or flip chart, or copies can be provided for the participants.

FSQ Interpretation: This two-page interpretive handout reviews each of the six guidelines for giving effective feedback, tying each to an item on the FSQ. A copy is needed for each participant.

Trainer Instructions

Purpose

This activity uses a brief, simple questionnaire to generate a self-assessment of feedback skills, leading to an in-depth group discussion of six guidelines for giving effective feedback. It is aimed at developing self-awareness and knowledge about effective feedback practices and does focus on not developing feedback skills.

Set-Up

Any number of people can be involved. A copy of the *Feedback Skills Questionnaire* (FSQ) will be needed for each participant. It will take about ten minutes for everyone to complete the FSQ, including time for giving instructions. Scoring takes a couple of minutes, but sharing scores can take fifteen to twenty minutes to set up, if everyone's scores are to remain anonymous. At least one half-hour should be allowed for discussion of the guidelines, and a full discussion of the results can easily take an hour.

It is important that the trainer carefully review the six guidelines for giving effective feedback (described in the handout) prior to the training session.

Steps

1. Explain that the Questionnaire about to be filled out is very simple and easy to "fake." If it is to have any value at all, participants must be as honest as possible in their responses. It is important to emphasize this, because the FSQ is "transparent" and susceptible to "desirability bias." That is, it is pretty obvious what kind of responses are "good" and what responses are not so good. Be sure to point out that individual scores will not be revealed.

2. Hand out the Questionnaires and allow about ten minutes for completion.

3. Have participants calculate their own scores by adding up the six numbers that were circled. Each person then writes his/her six item scores and the total on a separate sheet of paper which is collected. Then, while the forms are being collected, review the scoring norms with the group and answer any questions.

4. If possible have someone tally the individual item score reports and the reports of total scores while the trainer is engaged in Step 3. Obtain average scores for each item and for the entire Questionnaire, and post these scores on a flip chart or chalkboard.

5. Review each item with the group, explaining the guideline for effective feedback to which the item refers. Encourage questions and discussion, particularly with respect to what one might do about an item with a low score.

Discussion Questions

1. In general, which guideline is performed best (according to this group)? Why?

2. Which guideline is followed least? Why?

3. Try to give good and poor examples involving each of the six guidelines. Discuss the contrasts.

Feedback Skills Questionnaire

Directions: Circle the number that best represents your own behavior in giving feedback. Try to be as honest as you can; you will not be asked to disclose specific responses or scores. Your responses are for your own analysis and will be worth more to you if they are accurate.

1. To what extent do you use terms like "excellent," "poor," "good," or "bad" when you give someone feedback?

1	2	3	4	5	6	7

    always use   sometimes use   rarely or never
    such terms   such terms   use such terms

2. How often do you provide specific examples or concrete details when giving feedback?

1	2	3	4	5	6	7

    rarely give   sometimes give   always give
    specific details   specific details   specific details

3. In general, do you first ask whether the other person wants feedback?

1	2	3	4	5	6	7

    assume feedback   sometimes check to see if   always check to see if
    is wanted   feedback is wanted   feedback is wanted

4. When you give someone feedback is it generally because you want to get a load off your chest?

1	2	3	4	5	6	7

    generally I "unload"   sometimes I "unload"   I rarely "unload"
    with feedback   by giving feedback   when I give feedback

5. Do you generally give feedback as soon as possible or do you usually wait for an appropriate time, such as an appraisal session?

1	2	3	4	5	6	7

    generally I wait   usually I give feedback close   I always give
    for a good time   to the time of the behavior   feedback immediately

6. When you give a person feedback is it quite clear what that person could actually do to make effective use of your feedback?

1	2	3	4	5	6	7

    feedback I give is not   feedback I give is sometimes   feedback I give is always
    usually focused on   focused on applications   focused on applications
    applications

FSQ Scoring Norms

The total of the scores on the six items is the respondent's Feedback Skill Score. Scores range from seven to forty-two. The mean (for graduate students in managerial training) is 26. A distribution and scale are shown below and can be used by respondents to compare their scores with those of the norm group and with those of others in the class.

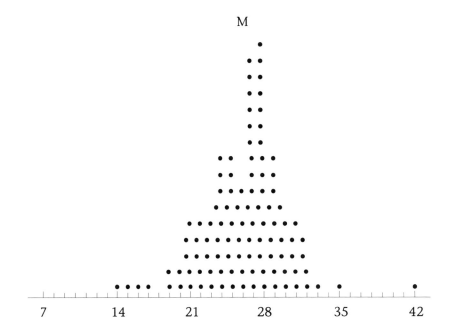

N	Mean (M)	Standard deviation	Range	Mode
107	26.2	4.02	14 – 36	28

Very high	31 and above
Above average	29 – 30
Average	24 – 28
Below average	22 – 23
Very low	21 and below

FSQ Interpretation

Each of the items on the FSQ is keyed to one of six basic guidelines for effective feedback. The six guidelines are shown below. We will briefly examine each guideline as it relates to each of the six items.

Guidelines for Helpful Feedback

1. Descriptive vs. Evaluative
2. Specificity vs. Generality
3. Needs of the Receiver vs. Needs of the Sender
4. Asked vs. Imposed
5. Timely vs. Out of Context
6. Applicable vs. Useless

Item 1: Descriptive versus Evaluative

Helpful feedback is descriptive, not evaluative. Evaluation — positive or negative — creates automatic blocks to effective communication. Effective descriptive feedback is also "owned"; it is clearly attributed to the describer, rather than presented as some omniscient pronouncement. "Your reaction to my comment seemed out of character and not at all like you," may be descriptive and is not overtly evaluative, yet a more effective statement would be, "Your reaction to my comment really surprised me, because I'd expected a very different response on the basis of our past contacts." The second statement, while it could be more specific, at least does not imply that the giver understands perfectly the "true" character of the receiver in some godlike fashion.

Item 2: Specificity versus Generality

Useful feedback is specific. If I am trying to help you learn Morse code and I say, "Your last message contained three errors," this is a descriptive comment and in itself not necessarily evaluative, but it is not specific enough to be of much help. "In your last message you substituted a 'P' for an 'L' once" is even less likely to be seen as evaluative and is specific enough to be useful — the receiver can practice A's, D's, P's, and L's. On a more inter-personal level the statement, "I saw your interactions with me in this group as being quite brief so that I didn't really understand what you were trying to say," is descriptive, non-evaluative, and owned by the giver. It is also far more general (and proportionately less helpful) than the statement, "Joe, you made that point about Bill's next assignment too quickly for me to grasp what you were getting at."

Item 3: Needs of the Receiver versus Needs of the Sender

Helpful feedback is given on the basis of the receiver's needs, not simply the needs of the sender to be heard or to "help." Such "help" is the kind of false help Gibb (1964) speaks of in a paper entitled, "Is Help Helpful?" This factor is closely related to the next one listed: is the feedback desired? Obviously, the recipient may not desire feedback yet may need it very much. In this case the helper has a difficult task, which is probably best begun by exploring with the receiver just why it is that he/she does not want feedback. It can also happen that the receiver may want feedback yet not appear to need it. In this case it would probably be easiest to give feedback and ask the recipient to explore why he/she feels a need for such feedback. Of course, the giver of feedback cannot ignore his or her own needs, but to give feedback solely on this basis without considering the needs of the receiver is not likely to be helpful to the receiver.

Item 4: Asked versus Imposed

Most of the time people *do* want feedback; the majority of us have learned that such information can be useful at times. It is also true that most of us could learn to make better use of feedback, yet the use (or disuse) we make of this information is also directly related to the manner and format in which it is given — the process of giving feedback. Most people give cues, verbal and nonverbal. We must always be attuned to and on the lookout for negative cues such as body position (turned away) or a verbal effort to redirect the conversation by the potential recipient. When such cues are perceived, it is then important to refrain from imposing feedback. If we consider the feedback particularly important or of great value at that moment, then we should always ask whether the feedback is permissible. This need not be done in so many words, but it should certainly be done. If the feedback is clearly not desired, we can try to explore why this is so.

Item 5: Timely versus Out of Context

Helpful feedback is of immediate relevance as seen by the recipient. Frequently this means that specific feedback is best given in the particular context in which the behavior that the feedback concerns took place and as soon after that behavior as possible. Naturally, this is not always true. It would be not only foolish but dangerous to give an automobile driver feedback on his steering wheel grip while he is concentrating on braking to avoid a rear-end collision. Such feedback could be useful after the car is safely stopped and the driver has calmed down. Accurate behavioral records, such as audio and videotape, can extend considerably the length of the period within which feedback is timely; these methods preserve much of the context. In general, however, the closer in time and context that the feedback is to the behavior on which it is based, the more helpful it will be.

Item 6: Applicable versus Useless

Useful feedback concerns behavior over which the recipient has some degree of control. The movie director tells the actor that his frequent eye blinks will distract viewers from the romance of the scene, but such feedback is pointless if the actor cannot control his eye blinks. The therapist may relate to his client the precise details of certain obsessive behaviors, but such feedback is useless if the client cannot control these behaviors. There are other types of useless feedback, for example, "You're so physically powerful that I'm afraid of you" is feedback the recipient cannot use directly, because few of us can change our physical appearance at will. A similar feedback statement is, "I tend to ignore advice from people with advanced educational degrees," when directed to an instructor with a Ph.D. These two examples illustrate cases in which the problem is the sender's not the receiver's and in which actions are more properly the responsibility of the sender. That is, the feedback could be helpful to the sender (for example, "How can I become more open to advice from people I categorize as my superiors?") but is not useful to the recipient. In general, then, feedback that cannot be used by the receiver fits the old saying "A difference that doesn't make any difference is no difference" and is not helpful.

Structured Activity   8

Developing
Feedback Skills

Summary

This activity is designed as a direct follow-up to Activity Seven, but it is possible to use this activity alone. Participants write brief cases about giving (or wanting to give) feedback. At this point the trainer presents the six guidelines for effective feedback. Participants are helped to score their *Feedback Skills Questionnaire* from Activity Seven (if used). Participants then analyze their written feedback cases in small groups and revise their feedback statements so that they follow the six guidelines. The final revised feedback statements are read to the entire group.

Contents

Trainer Instructions: Contains purpose, details of the set-up, step-by-step instructions for conducting the activity, and discussion questions.

Trainer Instructions

Purpose

This activity is designed to provide practice in constructing feedback using the six guidelines for giving effective feedback.

Set-Up

An unlimited number of small groups of three to four persons may participate. A large room with moveable chairs will be very helpful. The only materials participants need are paper and pencil. It will also be useful for participants to have with them copies of the *Feedback Skills Questionnaire* and the "Interpretation" handout.

It is strongly recommended that this activity only be used *after* the previous structured activity (Assessing Feedback Skills). If it is used without participants having completed the FSQ and engaging in a discussion of the six guidelines for giving effective feedback, then the trainer will have to spend at least one half-hour presenting a lecturette on the six guidelines.

Steps

1. Ask each person to think of a problem situation involving another person — something that happened during the past two or three months. Then, participants think of the feedback they would have *liked* to give the other person — regardless of whether they actually did so. Finally, each person writes down the feedback he/she would have liked to give. Allow ten minutes for this.

2. Present (or review) the six guidelines for giving effective feedback (from the "Interpretation" handout for the FSQ): descriptive; specific; directed to the receiver's needs; desired; timely; and applicable.

3. Form small groups of three or four people. Groups need not all be the same size. Each group member reads his/her feedback statement to the others in the group. The other group members critique the statement in terms of the six guidelines. Group members should point out how the statement could be revised so as to meet the guidelines.

4. After twenty minutes (or when most of the small groups have finished Step 3), stop the discussions and ask the participants to revise the feedback statements they had prepared, using the critiques of their peers. This should be done in writing. Allow ten minutes.

5. After ten minutes, ask the participants to review their revised statements within their small groups, to make sure that their revisions now fit the six guidelines for giving effective feedback. Allow ten minutes.

6. Stop the discussions. Bring the group back together and ask for volunteers to read their first and final revised statements. Ask for comments on the final revised statements: Does this statement meet the guidelines? If not, how might the statement be changed? Provide suggestions and guidance for improving the final statements, as needed.

7. Have a brief final review and concluding/summary discussion with the entire group.

Discussion Questions

1. How close to the guidelines were the "first tries"? Why were there such large discrepancies between the participants' statements and the guidelines?

2. Did the final revisions generally need further work?

3. Compare first attempts with final revisions. Would the recipient of the feedback react differently to the two versions? How? Why?

Structured Activity 9

Transparent Management

Summary

This role play is used to explore the consequences of poor hierarchical communication practices. It illustrates quite vividly what happens when a manager passes on a directive from above while letting his/her employees know that he/she really does not agree with the directive but must pass it along. Thus, the manager is transparent; passing a message on down the line as light passes through a window. The role play makes it clear how transparent management practices can destroy the effectiveness of both upward and downward communication.

Contents

Trainer Instructions: Contains purpose, details of the set-up, step-by-step instructions for conducting the activity, and discussion questions.

Role for Chris Reeves, Trainer: Gives role instructions for the "subordinate" in a two-person role play.

Role for Stacy Adams, Director of Training: Gives role instructions for the "supervisor" in a two-person role play.

"Transparent Management" Reading: Handout for participants explaining the concept of transparent management.

Trainer Instructions

Purpose

This activity is an unusually powerful exploration of the dynamics of upward and downward communication in organizations. One of the most difficult management situations occurs when one is faced with a decision made at a higher level, with which one is in basic disagreement. How does a mid-level manager deal with his/her own employees in a case like this? What are the alternatives and their consequences? The effect of a mid-level manager's overt — or subtle — refusal to support higher-level decisions is shown to "poison the well." Such refusal damages not only the organization's communication structure but can backfire and result in the manager being seen as untrustworthy and powerless by his/her employees. Trainers should review the two-page reading handout carefully, but it should not be assigned or given to participants until after the training session.

Set-Up

Any number of people may be involved. The activity takes place in pairs; if there is an odd number, the extra person can be an observer.

The activity usually takes at least an hour; an hour and one half would be typical, including time for group discussion.

Because each participant will play one of the roles, you will need enough copies to go around. No other materials are needed other than a flip chart and markers (or a chalkboard) to record and display the outcomes.

The training room should be large enough to permit multiple role play conversations at the same time without pairs being too close for "private" discussions. Moveable chairs will make the set-up much easier.

The activity can be conducted as an "on stage" role play with a single pair playing the roles and being observed by the rest of the group. The multiple role play format is recommended, because the participants are likely to learn and retain more if they experience the situation actively rather than passively.

Steps

1. Divide the participants into two groups. Give one group the role sheets for Chris Reeves and ask them to step outside of the room to read and prepare for their role.

2. Ask the remaining people to each take two chairs and set them in pairs scattered around the room. Then, each occupy one of their chairs. Give them the role sheets for Stacy Adams to read and prepare.

3. Check with each group to answer any questions about their role, without revealing any of the role information about the opposing role player.

4. Each Reeves will now enter the room, imagining that he/she is entering the office of Stacy Adams — the boss. Each will walk toward and be greeted by one of the Adams role players and will take the seat next to Adams.

5. Have the pairs begin the role play. Allow ten to fifteen minutes for the discussions.

6. Give a two-minute warning when half or more of the pairs seem to be finishing their discussions. Encourage everyone to "wrap it up" and then end the discussions, whether or not every pair is finished.

7. Ask each Reeves, in turn, to state what he/she thinks or understands to be the primary reason or issue underlying the meeting with Adams. Summarize the responses on the flip chart or chalkboard (leaving room beside each one for later responses from the Adamses).

8. When all of the Reeveses have answered, go back to the first pair and ask Adams to report what, if any, agreement was reached at the end of the discussion. The trainer should ask the Adamses not to reveal any details of their role at this time but to simply state, as briefly as possible, any agreements that were reached between the partners.

9. By the time all of the Adams role players have responded it will probably be clear that some of the pairs had different kinds of discussions. Explain that all Reeveses and all Adamses had exactly the same roles; there were no "secret" differences among those who took the roles. Return to the flip chart and put each pair's role play discussion into one of two categories based on the manner in which Adams addressed the underlying issue of the meeting — either blaming or not blaming upper management for the existing problem.

10. Focus now on the pairs in which the issues were addressed as problems created by upper-level managers. Compare them with pairs in which the issues were addressed but were not blamed on demands from above. Ask the Reeveses in these two categories how they now feel about upper management and contrast these feelings for the two categories. (Typically, the Reeveses feel negative toward higher-level managers when Adams lays the blame for the problem on management. Reeveses who participated in dealing with the problem but without Adams assigning blame to higher levels typically feel neutral or positive toward higher-level management.) Finally, ask some of the Reeveses in each category how they think *Reeves* would feel now about *Adams*. (Reeves role players who were told by Adams that the problem was due to higher-level managers' unreasonable demands will usually admit that Reeves probably does not think much of Adams at this point.) It is important to help the participants get out of their roles by asking that your questions be answered from the perspective of Reeves or Adams, not from the perspective of the participant him/herself. An open discussion of this point will also help to demonstrate that the negative

effects of transparent management can filter down to and backfire on the very person using it to escape responsibility for a difficult problem or decision. This is often a major insight for those playing the role of Adams.

11. Conclude with a description of transparent management and a group discussion of its nature and dangers (see the reading handout for details).

Discussion Questions

1. Is transparent management ever justified?

2. Can a manager change and decide to stop using transparent management? What effects would you expect in terms of the perceptions of his / her employees?

3. To what extent do the organizations that participants are familiar with have transparent management problems? Are certain types of organizations more (or less) likely to have such problems? Why?

Role for Chris Reeves, Trainer

You have been a trainer for the Killeen Manufacturing Company for over a year now. You have a bachelor's degree in business and worked in the personnel field for two years prior to this job. Most of your work has been training new hires for line jobs, using work simulations ("vestibule" training).

A couple of months ago your boss, Stacy Adams, announced a new policy: trainers would be encouraged to get into new training areas, to "diversify" rather than continue to specialize so much. This really turned you on. You had been starting to feel "stale," doing the same thing over and over again. Now you would have a chance to really show what you could do.

Adams was very supportive and gave you all the help you needed on your first new assignment, a two-day management development workshop. All-in-all it went well; Adams reviewed it in detail with you and showed you where you needed to do more design work and so on. Overall, though, you felt that the boss was really pleased with your performance, and your feeling was confirmed when Adams asked you to prepare for another one next month. You are really enthusiastic about the opportunity and plan to do even better than last time.

Adams just called you and asked if you could come by this afternoon to talk; you believe Adams probably wants to review your plans for the new workshop.

Role for Stacy Adams, Director of Training

You head up the training division of the Personnel Department of Killeen Manufacturing Company. You have a staff of seven trainers, along with a clerical/secretarial support group of three persons. Your unit is responsible for all training in a corporation of approximately 850 employees. This ranges from job training for newly-hired line workers to executive development for the top management group. In order to cover the diverse set of training activities, you have had specific trainers specialize in certain areas. Lately, however, you had the feeling that your staff might be getting too narrowly focused, and to remedy this you decided to offer them the opportunity to take on more varied assignments. Everyone was very positive about this approach, and they all expressed strong support.

Therefore, you offered the opportunity to design and run a management development workshop to Chris Reeves, a bright, young trainer you hired last year who has been doing "vestibule" training of line workers. Chris was delighted and said that this was a real chance for professional growth. You provided plenty of background and resource materials, but let Chris do the actual design work. You answered Chris' questions and felt the final design was sound.

Chris did the two-day workshop three weeks ago. The evaluations were positive but not outstanding. This did not upset you, as it is only normal to need some practice and to improve as a result. Basically, the workshop went well, with only one of the twelve managers having a particularly negative response. You did a good "post mortem" with Chris and felt that the next workshop Chris ran would be certain to get "outstanding" ratings.

Unfortunately, the disgruntled participant had a much worse reaction than you had realized. He wrote a strong letter to his corporate vice president complaining about the "aimless waste of time and money" in which he had participated. Apparently he felt that the skill-centered activities had no real point, purpose, or benefit. The VP came down on the Director of Personnel, who called you in. Actually, he was not angry, especially after you filled him in on the details. After all, these things occasionally happen. He did, however, insist that all future management development workshops incorporate a daily schedule outline, with specific goals stated for each workshop event, and with events specified on an hourly schedule. The schedule would be given to all participants prior to the workshop. You realize that this is a ridiculous approach, but he explained that he had to require it to appease his boss, the corporate VP. In particular, he noted that Chris' workshops should receive special attention in this regard. You gave him your best arguments against this decision but could not budge him. Now, it is up to you to tell Chris, who is preparing another management development workshop for next month. You just called and asked Chris to drop by this afternoon.

Transparent Management

The term "transparent management" describes something we see all too often in organizations: using higher-level demands to justify what "we have to do" (or appear to do). For example, a corporate vice president, outraged by a complaint from a manager about the value of a recent training workshop, may tell the personnel director, "From now on I want a detailed schedule for every one of the workshops!" The personnel director tells the training director: "I know it's foolish and a waste of time, but the VP just doesn't understand the nature of training. Let's just play along as best we can." The training director, who knows just how much wasted effort the trainers are in for, then tells them, "I'm sorry about this new requirement. It's certainly not my idea; in fact, I fought it as hard as I could. It's really due to that numbskull VP!" In other words, the personnel director and the training director have acted like panes of glass, passing the VP's "foolish" directive down to the trainers, emphasizing that it is quite unrelated to them: they are "transparent," and therefore, blameless.

This situation is acceptable to them, *for now*. But what are the longer-range implications of this behavior, this transparent management? Obviously, it does not encourage confidence in the judgment of higher levels of management. When one's boss refers to his or her own superiors as "numbskulls," or uses less offensive labels such as ill-informed, stubborn, or political, this conveys a clear lack of confidence. Certainly one instance of this does not tarnish the images of all top managers; it is when transparent management occurs with some frequency that such a negative image is developed.

There are, however, some consequences of transparent management that are far more significant than a tarnished image. There are consequences with respect to the process of upward communication in the organization. Specifically, employees are not likely to pass information upward that has no effect, is rejected, or results in negative outcomes for them. Thus, in the example just discussed, both the trainer and his / her boss will be less likely to inform "higher-ups" of what is happening with respect to management development training. Rather, they will follow the new rules and file the schedules — schedules that will be designed to create minimal inconvenience for the trainers, while satisfying top management's new rule, but not to communicate the details or intent of the training to potential participants.

What is the trainer likely to think of his or her boss? And what does that person think about those at the next level? Both are likely to develop an image of a low-power, ineffectual manager who has little influence upward in the organization. How does one deal with such people? Typically, if an employee wants to get ahead, such low-power individuals are bypassed, receive little (or inaccurate) information, and are seen as hindrances to be overcome. Notice that this is how the trainer comes to see (and act toward) his or her boss as well as describes how the trainer's boss begins to view the person at the next level up. Communication and trust are systematically stifled and poisoned between each level, not just between the top and lower levels. In fact, the organization's "climate" — that hard-to-pin-down yet very real atmosphere that behavioral scientists like Likert (1967) or Harrison (1972) point to as affecting such concrete outcomes as costs, productivity, and profits — is profoundly affected for the worse.

Transparent management is the easy way out. It relieves one of responsibility for unpopular decisions while making sure that the decisions are (or appear to be) carried out. However, despite the short-run gain, the long-run effects are very dangerous. How can transparent management be avoided?

Avoiding transparent management requires that managers at all levels be comfortable in openly expressing disagreements with their superiors. Of course, this is easier said than done, and the existence of a transparent management syndrome would make such open discussions quite unlikely. In some organizations, however, boss and subordinate managers do discuss disagreements — just as in the brief case discussed earlier — and the transparent management syndrome still exists. Open confrontation or disagreement is necessary, but not itself sufficient to prevent transparent management. Real prevention requires a certain stance on the part of subordinate managers.

To avoid transparent management, disagreements must be resolved in one of several ways:

- the subordinate and superior may develop a new decision that both can support;

- the subordinate may be convinced of the correctness of the superior's decision and support it, or vice versa, the boss may be convinced;

- the subordinate may conclude that the superior's decision is incorrect but still manageable, and supportable on that ground (and must make it clear to the boss that this is the subordinate's open viewpoint);

- the subordinate may conclude that the superior's decision is wrong and damaging, and cannot be supported, in which case the subordinate must request a transfer or resign.

This last alternative sounds harsh at first and people may think, "You mean that whenever I think the supervisor's decision is wrong I've got to resign? You're kidding — I'd be resigning ten times a day!" That, however, is not a valid inference, because our third option says, in effect, "Well, I really think this is the wrong way to go, but I admit that you might be right and I don't think any real damage will be done, regardless, so I'll support this action *as my own.*" In other words, the subordinate "buys into" the boss' decision with their disagreement open and understood. In real life this is by far the more common outcome than the fourth alternative, because, in reality, very few decisions are likely to have such negative results as to be unsupportable.

What if alternative four is called for but is unacceptable for economic or other reasons? This is then an ethical question for the subordinate. It seems clear, though, that using transparent management in such a case only makes a bad situation worse for the organization.

How can transparent management be "cured"? Clearly this is a more difficult matter than prevention. The only effective treatment is probably organizational, because the problem is organizational. A variety of actions seem feasible. For example:

- survey and feedback sessions throughout the organization using the small work group "waterfall" design pioneered by Mann (1957);

- management training workshops for all managers, focused on superior-subordinate communication and emphasizing confrontation of conflicts (Walton, 1969) and integrative problem solving (Morris and Sashkin, 1976);

- "process consultation" throughout the organization, in the manner of Schein (1969);

- "third-party consultation" applied at critical points throughout the organization, as detailed by Walton (1969).

Certainly there are other possible change actions that could help reverse a climate of transparent management. But prevention is easier and less costly and deserves emphasis. In general, the loss of a weak crutch like transparent management is a step toward increased organizational health and effectiveness.

References

Gibb, J. R. "Is Help Helpful?"

Harrison, R. "Understanding Your Organization's Character." *Harvard Business Review*, 1972, 50, (4), pp. 119–128.

Likert, R. *The Human Organization.* New York: McGraw-Hill, 1967.

Mann, F. C. "Studying and Creating Change: A Means to Understanding Social Organization." In C. M. Arensberg, et al. (eds.), *Research In Industrial Human Relations.* New York: Harper, 1957. (Industrial Relations Research Association Publication Number 17)

Morris, W. C., & Sashkin, M. *Organization Behavior in Action.* St. Paul, MN: West, 1976.

Schein, E. H. *Process Consultation.* Reading, MA: Addison-Wesley, 1969.

Walton, R. *Interpersonal Peacemaking.* Reading, MA: Addison-Wesley, 1969.

Suggested Readings

Gibb, J. R. "Defensive Communication." *Journal of Communication.* 1961, 11, pp. 141–148.

Jourard, S. M. *The Transparent Self* (2nd ed.). New York: Van Nostrand Reinhold, 1972.

Rogers, C. R., & Roethlisberger, F. J. "Barriers and Gateways to Communication." *Harvard Business Review*, July–August 1952, p. 46+.

Structured Activity   10

Trust —
The President's
Decision

Summary

Several years ago a researcher showed that when the statement, "the parties involved had a lot of confidence and trust in one another," was buried in a rather lengthy and difficult role play case, the groups were able to develop more effective solutions than when the trust issue was left unmentioned. He also found that when the opposite statement was added — telling participants that the trust level was very *low* among the group members — the quality of the solutions went down dramatically. This role play has been rewritten and simplified to reduce the study time required of participants, but the results are typically the same: participants in the "high trust" groups do quite well resolving the problem, while participants in the "low trust" groups never solve it. Most interesting of all, the participants in neither group figure out just why some groups do better than others — until they are shown the difference in the roles.

Contents

Trainer Instructions: Contains purpose, details of the set-up, and step-by-step instructions for conducting the activity.

Background Information: This material gives the role players some necessary background information about the situation; it may be handed out or read to the group.

Role Sheets: There are four roles in this exercise, but the roles are written in two different ways, so there are actually two *sets* of four roles. There is also a set of instructions for observers.

Case Analysis: A brief summary of the essential issues in this role play case is provided for the trainer. This information would not usually be handed out but would form the basis for the trainer's guidance of the post-activity discussion.

Trainer Instructions

Purpose

This activity involves groups of four people with each person playing the role of one of the top executives of a company. They are discussing what to do about a critical organizational problem. Two different sets of role instructions lead members in some groups to feel a high degree of trust in one another, while the members of the other groups feel great distrust toward one another. (One set of roles is coded A, the other is coded B.) This distinction leads to dramatic differences in outcomes. The underlying issue of trust and how trust and distrust are communicated often leads to significant insights on the part of group members with respect to interpersonal communication in groups.

Set-Up

While any number of groups of four can be involved, it is best if there are equal numbers of high- and low-trust groups, and it is helpful if there are at least two groups of each type. Because each group should also have an observer, this means that the ideal number of participants should be at least twenty. This is not a rigid rule; if necessary it is quite possible to have just two groups. If there are too few people to make up a third or fourth group, the role of Haney (vice president of personnel) can be omitted.

The room should be large enough that groups do not interfere with one another in terms of physical space or noise; break-out rooms are most desirable, if available. At least two hours are needed for this exercise, including time for debriefing and discussion.

Steps

1. Explain that the group members will be asked to play the roles of top executives of a manufacturing firm. Note that they should read over their roles carefully and try to assume the characteristics of the role as much as possible but should act as they actually would if they were put in this situation. (For example, one person is an electrical engineer, another a CPA, a third a Vietnam veteran.)

2. Form groups of five; if necessary, one or two groups may have only four members—no observer. Assign roles to the group members. Group members are to read only their own roles and are asked not to share the information on their role sheets except in the context of the role play discussion. Allow about five minutes for role preparation.

3. Explain that the groups will have about twenty to thirty minutes for this role play. Remind the participants that the observer (for groups that have one) is to be completely ignored. Emphasize that they are not to look at their own role sheets once the activity begins; give them two or three minutes at this time for a final review of their roles.

4. Role players are to fold their role information sheets in half into desk nameplates (text folded to the inside) and write their role names on the nameplates so that each of the group members can easily see the names. (This also makes it harder for group members to reexamine their role information sheets.) Remind the group members that they are to act as they would if they were in this situation, given the conditions described. If they forget any of the role information, they are not to review the role information sheets but are to make up reasonable information or answers as needed.

5. Begin the role play. Circulate among the groups to get a sense of how the discussions are proceeding and to determine when most of the groups are finished. When half of the groups are either finished or at a stalemate, tell the participants that they will have five more minutes.

6. Stop the action. Ask each "president," in turn, for the final decision or solution the group arrived at, and post this (in summary form) on a flip chart or chalkboard. When all of the solutions are posted go around the room again, asking observers to confirm and/or elaborate on the conclusion reached in their groups. Finally, ask the three vice presidents in each group whether they (a) support or oppose the decision, and (b) expect it to succeed or to fail.

7. It is probable that by this time everyone will realize that the president's decision (or initial position) regarding expansion — that is, not to expand — was based on the ultimatum delivered by the board of directors. Ask observers to confirm whether or not this fact was shared with the vice presidents by the president, and note this on the flip chart or chalkboard. Ask observers and group members why the information was or was not shared. Try to get some detail as to the discussion process for the high- and the low-trust groups, contrasting the two without pointing out the trust difference.

8. In concluding this exploration of the groups' discussions, focus on whether the president really gave the vice presidents a chance to work on the true problem. Ask each president why he/she presented the situation the way he/she did. Finally, ask one of the high-trust role players to read his or her role; stop the reader at the description of trust among the group members. Then ask one of the low-trust role players to read the same role section. Discuss the high- versus the low-trust issue. Explain that while high trust may not guarantee a good solution, low trust does guarantee that there will be no effective solution. Discuss with the entire group how management teams can develop trust.

Background Information

Air-Tronics, Inc. was established to produce radar equipment (communications and air-control gear, in particular) for the US Government. Most of their work was on government contracts, and the company did very well during the Vietnam War era. During that time they began to expand and move into the commercial electronics field, both in aviation and in consumer electronics. The company started to produce a variety of electronic parts and components for use in aircraft, televisions, stereo systems, and home appliances.

When the Vietnam War ended, much of the government work was eliminated, and ATI was forced to rely more and more on its commercial product line. However, they met stiff competition in both the aviation and the consumer electronics areas, from such industry giants as GE and RCA. To compete successfully ATI had to focus on a few products that were in general demand, manufacturing these at the lowest cost possible and selling in quantity and with a razor-thin profit margin. The firm's main profits came from single orders for specific items that were designed to the specifications of a particular customer and manufactured in relatively small quantity. Therefore, ATI had to have the ability to respond quickly to customer needs and to make rapid changes in production. This called for skilled and creative engineers and for production people who could adapt quickly to frequent changes, solving problems while constantly seeking to minimize costs. For several years the company struggled to survive, without any substantial progress. The firm was clearly in trouble in just about every area, with the exception of the vice president for marketing who had some success in developing a salesforce that could land big "regular" orders while cultivating special order business and generating some market attention.

It was then that the Board of Directors decided to take drastic action. The president and the vice president for manufacturing were dismissed. The director of finance was made chief executive officer, and the production director was promoted to vice president for production. The personnel director was also promoted to vice president for human resources. Only the vice president for marketing was left in the same position. The Board felt that this group should be capable of turning the situation around. After two years, however, it was clear that while the situation was somewhat improved there was no dramatic change or turnaround.

Gale Clinton is the president and chief executive officer of Air-Tronics. Clinton is thirty-nine years old, holds a bachelor's degree in business from a good university, and is a Certified Public Accountant (CPA). For several years Clinton was ATI's comptroller, providing financial advice to management.

Chris Cable is vice president for human resources. Chris is forty years old and has been with ATI for almost twenty years, starting as a supervisor. After completing a bachelor's degree, Chris received several promotions, culminating in promotion to vice president. Chris has been responsible for all personnel functions for several years now.

Kit Donagal is vice president for production. Kit started as a line worker, volunteered for duty in Vietnam, and rejoined the company after returning. Donagal received regular promotions and became superintendent of a plant manufacturing government contract equipment. When that plant was closed, Donagal was made production director in one of ATI's main facilities. Kit is forty-three years old and has taken two years of college-level coursework in engineering and production management.

Jan Elden has been vice president for marketing for four years. Hired by the previous management, Jan had been assistant sales manager of a division of a much larger firm. Elden is thirty-eight years old and has an MBA with a major in marketing.

(A) Role for Gale Clinton, Chief Executive Officer

You have been president of ATI for the past two years. Before that you were the company's comptroller and gave financial advice to the former president. You are thirty-nine years old, hold a bachelor's degree in business, and you are a CPA. Your previous position helped you to understand the nature of the president's job, which is much more complex and broader in scope than your prior role in the company.

For the past year you and your vice presidents have been working on the issue of expansion as part of your efforts to turn the company around. Some of the advice you have heard has been negative — that real estate and construction costs are too high, and that new equipment costs are higher than the company can afford. All three of the vice presidents have come to favor expansion. You have kept an open mind, looking at all viewpoints, and were coming to the conclusion that a carefully planned and managed expansion would be the best course of action.

However, the company's Board of Directors summoned you late yesterday to a special meeting. They informed you that the company's performance was not acceptable and that they had expected better results from you. They told you that they had voted to give you one more year to show some significant results. If by that time the company is not in a much better financial condition, they will expect your resignation.

The Board's action took you by surprise. Expansion seems out of the question if you must show results within a year; it would take longer than that just to complete the financial arrangements required to build a new plant. The only possible course of action is to tighten up, contain costs, and try to show substantial improvement over the coming year.

You have called a meeting with your vice presidents to announce your decision. You have tried to work with them as a team over the past two years, giving them a voice in all major decisions. This has really paid off, and the group has been very effective in working together, with their interaction characterized by high trust and open communication. It is your hope and expectation that this will be a basis for the team to support you on the decision not to expand. You will, of course, review the issue with them to make sure that you have not overlooked any important facts in arriving at the decision not to expand.

(A) Role for Chris Cable, Vice President for Human Resources

You are forty years old and have been with the company for almost twenty years. You started as a supervisor, continued your education, and eventually earned your bachelor's degree in business administration. Two years ago you were promoted from personnel director to vice president. All of the usual personnel services, such as recruitment, hiring, promotions, training, and contract negotiations are handled through your office.

You are proud of the program you started for hiring and training promising new college recruits. This has added several good new people each year over the past four years. When top management was replaced two years ago your recruits were able to move up in the organization. Recently, however, the company has not been growing as you had expected, and there has been no place for your new crop of management trainees to go. Without promotion potential it is difficult to hold on to the best employees and harder still to recruit the best new graduates. You feel especially bad that your competitors are getting the people you had hoped would represent the future of your company.

In your view expansion would provide the room for advancement that is critically needed for the company's success in the long run. You have let Gale Clinton, the president, know how you feel; you think Gale has been listening and is favorable. Clinton does not like to make quick decisions, especially on major issues like the question of expansion. Gale generally tries to involve the entire top management team in open discussion of such issues and in making important decisions. The top managers work well together as a team, far better than the previous group ever did. Everyone seems to have a great deal of trust toward the others, and this helps you to work effectively as a group. You are hopeful that today's top management meeting is for a final review and approval of the decision to expand.

(A) Role for Jan Elden, Vice President for Marketing

You have been vice president for marketing for four years. Before you came to the company you were an assistant sales manager of a division of a much larger company. You are thirty-eight years old, have an MBA with a major in marketing, and are the only member of the previous management team who was not asked to resign. Before you came the company had no real sales organization, so you took the opportunity to build a whole new sales staff and organization. It was hard work but you have been successful, and that is why you were asked to stay on when the management was changed by the Board of Directors.

You set up sales offices in all of the major eastern cities and were able to build up the company's market. You were given even more leeway by Clinton, the new president, and this has been helpful. Your greatest current problem is your inability to deliver on big orders due to the physical plant limitations. You have been pressing Gale to approve the type of expansion you feel is critical if the company is to grow and profit. As it is, Donagal, the vice president for production, often tells you that the deadline to be met (to successfully get a big order) is just not possible due to the limits on plant facilities. With a new, modern plant there would be no excuses, and you could accept more of the big, profitable orders that you now lose to competitors who can better meet clients' delivery needs. This new set-up would also help spur new product development which is critical for developing future business.

Clinton has been receptive to your arguments, and you have reason to believe that the top management meeting called for this afternoon will center on the decision to go ahead with the expansion; at least, you hope that is the case. Unlike the previous chief executive, Clinton always involves the top management group in such major decisions. Over the past two years you have learned to work together very effectively; there is a lot of openness and trust among the top managers, and this helps when you are faced with a major decision like expansion.

(A) Role for Kit Donagal, Vice President for Production

You have worked for ATI since high school, starting as a line worker and working your way up to the executive ranks. Along the way you spent a year in Vietnam and completed two years of college courses in engineering and production management. You are now forty-three years old and were promoted to your present position two years ago when the management group was changed by the Board of Directors. You are very familiar with the company, having started your career in one of the old government contract facilities (now long shut down), and most recently have been production director in one of ATI's main facilities.

When you became a vice president you hoped to make some major changes in equipment and operations. The former management was not willing to invest in equipment and facilities and this was part of their downfall. Clinton, the new president, has been willing to make some of the changes you recommended, and the improvements have been of great benefit. However, you have done just about as much as is humanly possible within the limits of the existing plant. ATI must have a new plant if it is to continue to improve operations. The present building is out of date, and the four-story structure makes some manufacturing operations difficult if not impossible. Maintenance is far more costly than in new, modern plants. Even if Clinton approved purchase of certain major new equipment you need, the equipment could not be put where it is needed due to the physical limits of the building.

You have told Clinton repeatedly of the need for an expanded new facility with up-to-date equipment. You are anxious that the decision be made soon. The President does not like to move quickly on such important matters and generally involves the entire top management group in such decisions. Over the past two years you have developed into a very effective team with a lot of confidence and trust in one another. This is a real contrast with the way the previous top team operated.

Clinton has called a meeting with all of the vice presidents. You are hoping that there will be a decision to take your advice and expand operations with a new plant facility; anyway, that's the way Clinton seemed to be leaning.

(B) Role for Gale Clinton, Chief Executive Officer

You have been president of ATI for the past two years. Before that you were the company's comptroller and gave financial advice to the former president. You are thirty-nine years old, hold a bachelor's degree in business, and you are a CPA. Your previous position helped you to understand the nature of the president's job, which is much more complex and broader in scope than your prior role in the company.

For the past year you and your vice presidents have been working on the issue of expansion as part of your efforts to turn the company around. Some of the advice you have heard has been negative — that real estate and construction costs are too high, and that new equipment costs are higher than the company can afford. All three of the vice presidents have come to favor expansion. You have kept an open mind, looking at all viewpoints, and were coming to the conclusion that a carefully planned and managed expansion would be the best course of action.

However, the company's Board of Directors summoned you late yesterday to a special meeting. They informed you that the company's performance was not acceptable and that they had expected better results from you. They told you that they had voted to give you one more year to show some significant results. If by that time the company is not in a much better financial condition, they will expect your resignation.

The Board's action took you by surprise. Expansion seems out of the question if you must show results within a year; it would take longer than that just to complete the financial arrangements required to build a new plant. The only possible course of action is to tighten up, contain costs, and try to show substantial improvement over the coming year.

You have called a meeting with your vice presidents to announce your decision. Over the past two years you have tried to work with them as a group, but you are not sure that they really trust one another — or you for that matter. The previous CEO was fired by the Board of Directors for poor financial results, and one of the current vice presidents might be hoping to take your job in the same manner.

In this meeting you plan to review the issue of expansion with the vice presidents to make sure that you have not overlooked any important facts in arriving at the decision not to expand. You hope to get the vice presidents to support you.

(B) Role for Chris Cable, Vice President for Human Resources

You are forty years old and have been with the company for almost twenty years. You started as a supervisor, continued your education, and eventually earned your bachelor's degree in business administration. Two years ago you were promoted from personnel director to vice president. All of the usual personnel services, such as recruitment, hiring, promotions, training, and contract negotiations are handled through your office.

You are proud of the program you started for hiring and training promising new college recruits. This has added several good new people each year over the past four years. When top management was replaced two years ago your recruits were able to move up in the organization. Recently, however, the company has not been growing as you had expected, and there has been no place for your new crop of management trainees to go. Without promotion potential it is difficult to hold on to the best employees and harder still to recruit the best new graduates. You feel especially bad that your competitors are getting the people you had hoped would represent the future of your company.

In your view expansion would provide the room for advancement that is critically needed for the company's success in the long run. You have let Gale Clinton, the president, know how you feel; you think Gale has been listening and is favorable. Clinton does not like to make quick decisions, especially on major issues like expansion. This is probably due in part to the general lack of openness and trust among the top managers. You think Clinton might be worried that one of the vice presidents is out to get the job of CEO; after all, Gale was promoted to fill the job of the former president when the Board of Directors fired the previous management group. Nonetheless, you are hopeful that today's top management meeting is for a final review and approval of the decision to expand.

(B) Role for Jan Elden, Vice President for Marketing

You have been vice president for marketing for four years. Before you came to the company you were an assistant sales manager of a division of a much larger company. You are thirty-eight years old, have an MBA with a major in marketing, and are the only member of the previous management team who was not asked to resign. Before you came the company had no real sales organization, so you took the opportunity to build a whole new sales staff and organization. It was hard work but you have been successful, and that is why you were asked to stay on when the management was changed by the Board of Directors.

You set up sales offices in all of the major eastern cities and were able to build up the company's market. You were given even more leeway by Clinton, the new president, and this has been helpful. Your greatest current problem is your inability to deliver on big orders due to the physical plant limitations. You have been pressing Gale to approve the type of expansion you feel is critical if the company is to grow and profit. As it is, Donagal, the vice president for production, often tells you that the deadline to be met (to successfully get a big order) is just not possible due to the limits on plant facilities. With a new, modern plant there would be no excuses, and you could accept more of the big, profitable orders that you now lose to competitors who can better meet clients' delivery needs. This new set-up would also help spur new product development which is critical for developing future business.

Clinton has been receptive to your arguments, and you have reason to believe that the top management meeting called for this afternoon will center on the decision to go ahead with the expansion; at least, you hope that is the case. You are not absolutely sure, because the other vice presidents are not very open with one another or with the president. There does not seem to be much trust among them. Maybe one of them is after the president's job; after all, Clinton is CEO now because of being in the right place to succeed the last president when he was fired by the Board of Directors.

(B) Role for Kit Donagal, Vice President for Production

You have worked for ATI since high school, starting as a line worker and working your way up to the executive ranks. Along the way you spent a year in Vietnam and completed two years of college courses in engineering and production management. You are now forty-three years old and were promoted to your present position two years ago when the management group was changed by the Board of Directors. You are very familiar with the company, having started your career in one of the old government contract facilities (now long shut down), and most recently have been production director in one of ATI's main facilities.

When you became a vice president you hoped to make some major changes in equipment and operations. The former management was not willing to invest in equipment and facilities and this was part of their downfall. Clinton, the new president, has been willing to make some of the changes you recommended, and the improvements have been of great benefit. However, you have done just about as much as is humanly possible within the limits of the existing plant. ATI must have a new plant if it is to continue to improve operations. The present building is out of date, and the four-story structure makes some manufacturing operations difficult if not impossible. Maintenance is far more costly than in new, modern plants. Even if Clinton approved purchase of certain major new equipment you need, the equipment could not be put where it is needed due to the physical limits of the building.

You have told Clinton repeatedly of the need for an expanded new facility with up-to-date equipment, but you are concerned that Gale just does not believe you. The four top managers do not seem to share confidence or trust in one another; they remember how just about all of the previous top managers were fired by the Board of Directors because of their inability to achieve the financial results expected by the Board. Of course, that is how Clinton came to be president; in fact you would not be surprised to hear that one of the other vice presidents hopes to succeed Clinton in the same way.

Clinton has called a meeting with all of the vice presidents. You are hoping that there will be a decision to take your advice and expand operations with a new plant facility; anyway, that's the way Clinton seemed to be leaning.

Instructions for Observers

You have heard or read the background information, so you know many facts about Air-Tronics, Inc. (ATI) and about the four top managers. While the facts of the case serve as important background, you must, in your job as observer of the group's "process," look beyond these facts to see how the people involved really think and feel and how they relate to one another. You should be on the lookout for indicators of feelings and relationships that may not be spoken openly. Try to read "between the lines"; do not be misled about what is going on by looking only at the overt "facts." Here are some guidelines to help you:

1. Watch how Gale Clinton starts the meeting. Is Clinton comfortable? How about the others? Did Clinton start out by defining a problem for discussion or present a solution, a final decision?

2. Why was this meeting called? Do you think there is some hidden or unstated reason?

3. How did the vice presidents respond to the president's introductory statements? Was the president open to their comments and views? Did Clinton appear to be on the defensive?

4. Would you say that the group members were working together to solve a problem? If not, why? What is the underlying problem in this case?

5. Did you see any of the participants acting frustrated or stubborn? Who? Why? Is there evidence that some of the participants felt fearful or threatened in the course of the discussion?

6. Was everyone open about the facts of the situation, or do you think some of the group members might have been withholding information or "playing their cards close to the vest"? What behaviors might indicate that a person was not sharing information completely?

7. If there was a final decision, do you think that everyone supports it? How satisfied do the participants appear with the results of the meeting?

Case Analysis

The President's Decision is a difficult role play as it was originally designed. It was intended to be a "capstone" activity at the conclusion of an advanced management development seminar. Solving the problem requires group members — including the president — to level with one another and work together to develop a plan to show the Board of Directors that their ultimatum (significant profits within a year) is impossible and will only ensure the destruction of the firm. But they are all somewhat afraid of losing their jobs, and it is easy to become defensive under such conditions. It is even easier to understand their fears when we recall that all but one of them were promoted into their present positions when the last set of top managers was fired by the Board under similar circumstances. (The only exception was the vice president for marketing, whose outstanding performance was recognized and who was retained.) If the role players have learned the skills of operating as a team — really listening to one another, for example, not just striving to win for one's own position, and seeking and sharing information to define the problem, rather than making assumptions and keeping secrets — then they can get to the heart of the problem and develop a realistic approach to resolve it. Whether this is the outcome depends on the extent and quality of the training as well as on the capacity of the participants. Sometimes only one out of five groups arrives at a high-quality solution.

The present version of this case, which has been substantially modified to update the context, is designed not as a "final exam" but to demonstrate the significant effects of trust on group problem solving. In 1972, Dale Zand, a well-known organization development consultant, as well as a researcher, published the results of a study he had conducted using a modified version of *The President's Decision*. Zand took the original roles (first published in 1957 by N. R. F. Maier and his associates) and prepared two slightly different versions. No changes were made in the basic content of the case, but in one version the role players were told the group had a history of working well together in an atmosphere of mutual respect and trust. In the other version, still with no change in content details, the role players were informed that the group members really did not trust one another at all, that some might even be out to "knife the others in the back." In both cases this information was buried in the roles and was not a central feature or focus. The results were dramatic.

Zand found that many of the groups in which the role players were told that they trusted one another arrived at creative, high-quality solutions. These results were much more frequent than when the trust aspect was not part of the role information. In other words, comparing the high-trust condition to the older version of the case, adding trust improved the outcomes substantially. The reverse was true when the new information concerned a lack of trust. Not a single group in which the members were told that they did not trust one another ever solved the problem! And, even more interesting, neither the high-trust nor the low-trust groups could understand why it was that some groups seemed to work effectively to solve the problem while others failed — until they were *told* about the different instructions with regard to trust. Then they felt it was obvious!

The present version of *The President's Decision* has been modified even further. The older versions are quite long and often work better if participants take their roles home to read beforehand. The present roles have been condensed for much shorter review time but with very little loss of content or detail. The high-trust roles are first (coded A), followed by the four low-trust versions (coded B).

Remember that the key to this case is the president's willingness — or failure — to trust his closest associates with the Board's bad news: that there is an ultimatum in effect, perform or leave. In the high-trust situation, Clinton will often take this risk because the president knows that all of them see the situation as one they face together as a team. In the low-trust situation, Clinton understandably fears that any one of the others might try to get the president's job, so it is only sensible to keep the real situation "under wraps." Of course, the vice presidents will still sense that there is something wrong, and they often conclude that Gale Clinton is hiding something from them. The situation often degenerates into frustration and argument.

The only way to solve this problem is for the president openly to tell the vice presidents about the Board's ultimatum and ask them for their ideas. Clinton must move them toward dealing with the real problem, which is not whether or not to expand, but how to respond to the ultimatum. There are two basic options: (1) figure out how to show a dramatic performance improvement within a year or (2) figure out how to convince the Board that their demands are impossible to meet. Most groups conclude that (2) is the only viable approach, but when approached directly as a problem to be solved, (1) may provoke creative responses.

It is extremely difficult to try to solve a problem in an atmosphere of threat and fear, yet this is what the absence of trust leads to typically. When the parties involved trust one another, they no longer need to be as fearful, and they can invest energy in looking for creative solutions to their mutual problems, rather than building defenses and protecting themselves. This is the essential lesson Jack Gibb tries to get across in his treatment of defensive and supportive communication climates (see Activity 11). The brief questionnaire in Activity 11 can be used here at the end of the role play and with the group members still playing their roles. This will provide clear, quantitative data about the differences in the communication climate of trust between the high- and low-trust groups.

Structured Activity   11

The Climate
of Communication

Summary

This activity centers on a brief, twelve-item survey that gets at the underlying "climate" of communication in a group, unit, or organization. The aim is not to diagnose an organization or group but to provide a platform for discussion of the six dimensions of communication climates. A brief handout or lecturette outline is provided, describing the six dimensions in terms originally defined by Jack Gibb in a classic article on "defensive communication." Gibb pointed out how organizations tended to be on one or the other end of a spectrum each defined by six dimensions. On one end the climate may encourage open, effective communication by being: descriptive, problem-oriented, spontaneous, empathic, equality-enhancing, and provisional. On the other end the climate may provoke strong defensiveness on the part of individuals by being: evaluative, solution-focused, strategy-based, effectively neutral, superiority-enhancing, and certain — thus hindering effective communication.

Contents

Trainer Instructions: Contains purpose, details of the set-up, and step-by-step instructions for conducting the activity.

Organizational Communication Climate Survey (OCCS): In this twelve-item survey participants are asked to describe the communication climate in their own unit (or organization). The OCCS is not intended as a valid assessment tool but as a vehicle for discussing the nature of supportive and defensive climates.

Organizational Communication Climate Survey — Scoring: Provides an explanation of how to score the OCCS for the six climate dimensions.

Organizational Communication Climate Survey — Interpretation: This is a brief explanation of the nature of organizational communication climates, summarizing Gibb's six underlying dimensions.

Trainer Instructions

Purpose

The *Organizational Communication Climate Survey* (OCCS) was designed to help participants understand the "climate" of interpersonal communication. The Survey generates data that participants can relate to because they are asked to describe their own unit or organization, but it is important to emphasize to participants that the OCCS is not considered to be a valid diagnostic instrument.

Set-Up

Although the OCCS might be used with an intact work unit or department, this would depend on a solid basis of trust and openness among the group members. It is recommended that the OCCS be used with participants who are not all part of the same work unit and that in answering the twelve items participants be asked to refer to the organization as a whole.

The OCCS can be used with any number of people. The activity will usually take about an hour, longer if (as a follow-up) participants are put into sub-groups to discuss specific dimensions and develop plans for improving the organization's scores.

Each participant needs a copy of the Survey and the "OCCS — Scoring" instructions; the "OCCS — Interpretation" sheet may be handed out or used as the basis for a lecturette on supportive and defensive communication climates.

Steps

1. Explain that the group is going to examine the nature of the communication climate in the organization. Hand out copies of the OCCS, one for each participant, and ask them to answer the twelve questions privately. Instruct them *not* to put their names on the forms; responses are to be anonymous. Allow ten to fifteen minutes for everyone to fill out the Survey.

2. Hand out the scoring instructions. Each participant will calculate his/her seven scores (the six dimensions and an overall score). Have each person write his/her scores on a separate piece of paper; collect these and prepare and post a distribution of scores.

3. Examine the average and range for each dimension, defining and explaining each dimension in order. Use the "OCCS — Interpretation" sheet to prepare your presentation, or look up Jack Gibb's article, "Defensive Communication," which you will find in the *Journal of Communication*, volume 11 (1961), pages 141 to 148. This journal can be found in almost all college or university libraries and in most large city libraries.

4. In a concluding group discussion, you might consider some or all of the following questions:

- On which of the six climate dimensions did most of the participants score high? On which did people typically rate the organization low? Why?

- Ask for examples of effective behavior for those dimensions that seemed to have the lowest scores.

- Ask for participants to try practicing some of the more difficult types of behavior that help develop a supportive communication climate. Discuss why it is difficult to use these behaviors and how one might learn to use them more effectively.

The last two of these questions might also be topics for small group activity and discussion.

Organizational Communication Climate Survey

Directions: This brief questionnaire refers to the nature of interpersonal communication in your work unit or organization. Answer each question in terms of the extent to which the people with whom you interact in your work unit or organization — employees, peers, and higher-level managers — typically display the behaviors described. You are not trying to evaluate any particular person; the aim is to get a "picture" of the overall "climate" of interaction in the work unit or organization.

Answer Key: VG = To a Very Great Extent
C = To a Considerable Extent
M = To a Moderate Extent
S = To a Slight Extent
LN = To Little or No Extent

Circle the letter(s) that best represent the extent to which you think the behavior described is common in your work unit or organization.

To what extent do people in this work unit / organization. . .

1.	show that they listen to one another; try to understand others' viewpoints?	VG	C	M	S	LN
2.	"pick up on" and verbally describe the feelings another member has and tries to express?	VG	C	M	S	LN
3.	ask others to repeat or clarify what they have said in order to better understand?	VG	C	M	S	LN
4.	restate for clarification what another person has said before going on to make their own points?	VG	C	M	S	LN
5.	share their own feelings in clear and non-threatening ways?	VG	C	M	S	LN
6.	provide support and encouragement in a discussion in order to really explore an issue in depth?	VG	C	M	S	LN
7.	give others a chance to talk; "opening the door" for others to contribute to a discussion?	VG	C	M	S	LN
8.	help explore an issue in depth without trying to push their own ideas?	VG	C	M	S	LN
9.	say clearly, "up front," what their expectations of one another really are?	VG	C	M	S	LN
10.	face disagreements directly; try to understand the reasons underlying differences?	VG	C	M	S	LN
11.	give one another feedback that is concrete and specific without being evaluative?	VG	C	M	S	LN
12.	when talking, care about another as a person and colleague?	VG	C	M	S	LN

Organizational Communication Climate Survey

Scoring

For every *VG* you circled give yourself five points. Give four points for each *C*, three points for each *M*, two points for each *S*, and one point for each *LN*. Add up all the points to get a Total Score for your work unit/organization. The higher the Total Score, the more the organization's communication climate approaches the supportive ideal; the lower the score, the more likely that the climate is defensive. Scores can range from a low of twelve to a high of sixty. The following guidelines may be helpful.

> 12–24 = Very Defensive Climate
> 25–36 = Somewhat Defensive Climate
> 37–48 = Somewhat Supportive Climate
> 49–60 = Very Supportive Climate

The OCCS also generates six subscores. Follow the instructions below to obtain your subscores for the six dimensions of organizational communication climate.

Description vs. Evaluation: Add the scores for OCCS items 2, 4, 9, and 11. High scores indicate a climate of description, low scores a climate of evaluation.

Problem Orientation vs. Control: Add the scores for OCCS items 3, 10, 11, and 12. High scores indicate a climate of problem orientation, low scores a climate of control.

Spontaneity vs. Strategy: Add the scores for OCCS items 5, 6, 8, and 9. High scores indicate a climate of spontaneity, low scores a climate of strategy.

Empathy vs. Neutrality: Add the scores for OCCS items 1, 2, 4, and 12. High scores indicate a climate of empathy, low scores a climate of neutrality.

Equality vs. Superiority: Add the scores for OCCS items 3, 5, 6, and 7. High scores indicate a climate of equality, low scores a climate of superiority.

Provisionalism vs. Certainty: Add the scores for OCCS items 1, 7, 8, and 10. High scores indicate a climate of provisionalism, low scores a climate of certainty.

Some rough guidelines for interpreting the subscale scores are as follows:

> 4–8 = Provokes Extreme Defensiveness
> 9–12 = Provokes Defensiveness
> 13–16 = Supportive
> 17–20 = Extremely Supportive

Organizational Communication Climate Survey

Interpretation

There has been much research on organizational communication over the past twenty-five years. One of the earliest, but most important, studies was by Dr. Jack Gibb who identified two basic types of climate for communication in organizations. He observed that in some organizations communication was generally open and accurate, that people got involved in solving organizational problems together, sharing and using information to deal with problems effectively. In other organizations it seemed as though people were almost afraid to talk to one another; problems were not dealt with effectively because no one was able to pull together the necessary information and get people involved and working together. Gibb called the first type of organizational communication climate "supportive," because people generally felt supportive toward one another and worked together to make the organization effective. This was accomplished in part through open, effective communication. The second type of climate was labelled "defensive" by Gibb. In such climates people protected themselves and did not help one another. They avoided communication in an effort to make sure they would not get the blame for anything going wrong.

Actually, the two communication climates identified by Gibb are the extreme points of a single climate dimension; most climates will fit somewhere in-between. Gibb found that over time each of the two basic climate types tended to reinforce itself so that most organizations would "drift" toward one end of the scale or the other; that is why the two climate types seem to be completely different and independent.

These communication climates consist of and are supported by six sub-dimensions. Again, Gibb was able to identify the opposite ends of each of these dimensions. We can look not only at the overall climate but can also examine it in more detail in terms of the six sub-dimensions. Let us look briefly at each.

Evaluation-Description: A defensive communication climate is created when people evaluate one another's behavior. This is true whether the evaluation is positive or negative; it is normal for people to feel threatened and fearful when they know they are being judged. But isn't evaluative information important and needed? Perhaps, but for the most part what is really essential is information that simply describes conditions as they are. Unfortunately, our everyday speech and interactions are so frequently judgment-oriented that we often find it difficult to be simply descriptive and avoid making implicit evaluations. Descriptive communication has two advantages: not only does it help maintain a supportive climate — avoiding reactions based on feelings of fear and threat — but it provides information instead of conclusions. Even if a judgment is accurate, it is not usually very useful for understanding a problem and developing possible solutions.

Control-Problem Orientation: A great many of our communication interactions are oriented toward obtaining some kind of control over the other person(s) involved. But people are surprisingly aware of attempts to control them, whether such efforts are obvious or subtle, and the normal reaction is to resist, to respond defensively. This is so much the case that when someone acts without such an intent, with a focus on working together to solve a mutual problem, people often assume that the individual simply is hiding his or her "real" intent! A problem orientation means that one really is not trying to "sell" his or her own solution by persuading or changing the other person. When the aim is to control others by imposing our solutions on them, there is a natural defensive reaction; the result is a defensive communication climate. When the goal is to work together to resolve a problem, without assuming that either party has "the" answer, one consequence is a supportive climate.

Strategy-Spontaneity: Most people react even more strongly to a controlling approach when they see it as part of a strategy, especially a hidden strategy. Reactions are often so negative that the underlying issue becomes blown out of proportion. When people are trying out hidden strategies on one another, the result is a defensive climate. In a supportive climate, on the other hand, most of us tend to be spontaneous; we do not rely on hidden plans. Instead we respond openly to the situation we see.

Neutrality-Empathy: A sense of not caring personally about others is both the cause and result of a defensive climate. After all, it does not make sense to become emotionally involved with people who might be your enemies. At the same time, such a stance provokes strong defensive reactions; we hear the neutral other communicating that we are not *worth* caring about, and that is deeply threatening. In contrast, in a supportive climate we tend to feel empathy toward one another; we seriously care about each other's feelings. This empathy does not imply agreement or sympathy, just understanding and respect. There is no better way to build a supportive communication climate than to express understanding of another person's feelings and thus to express the attitude that the other person is valued and worthy of concern.

Superiority-Equality: We typically react defensively to people who communicate to us that they are superior in some way, because we feel inadequate. And we often turn off whatever it is such people are trying to communicate. This approach arouses defensiveness because the "superior" person is saying that we are not equals, that the relationship is not one of mutual problem solving but is one in which the "superior" person has control and is going to "help" the inferior person. In contrast, supportive climates are characterized by feelings of equality and of not having to prove that one person is better than another. This does not mean that one person is not more talented, more beautiful, of higher status, or not more powerful than another; these are facts of life. But in a supportive climate, such facts are not central to the interaction, because, for the purpose of that particular interaction, the parties are choosing to act on a basis of equality.

Certainty-Provisionalism: In a defensive climate we typically feel very certain about our own positions. We also usually feel certain that the other person is "wrong." The other person, however, may conclude that we are really hiding inner feelings of uncertainty and that we have a need to appear certain and correct, whether we are or not. This leads to a rein-forcing spiral of greater and greater defensiveness. In contrast, supportive communication climates are generated when we are willing to suspend judgment, to take things "provision-ally," gathering data and testing facts to gain a better understanding of the situation. In a supportive climate people feel comfortable without having all the answers and are willing to share in the search for answers.

An organization's communication climate is the result of assumptions people make about the nature of the situation. The climate is created directly by the behaviors which people choose to engage in based on those assumptions. While it is not easy to change the organ-ization's communication climate, it is possible to change one's own actions. Understanding the six climate dimensions we have just defined can help. Keep in mind that each pair of labels we have been using (evaluation-description, etc.) are attached to the end points of a single dimension. The climate can be anywhere between these end points for any given situation as measured in terms of the six behavior dimensions. By analyzing the climate in terms of each dimension, we may be able to identify which dimension is contributing most to defensiveness and work to change that dimension while taking advantage of any others that are already more supportive than defensive. Of course, the more the overall climate is defensive, the harder it will be to communicate effectively — or to produce any change.

Structured Activity 12

Bob, Carol, Ted and Alec

Summary

This activity can be linked to most of the skills that are covered in the other structured activities in this book. Bob, Carol, Ted and Alec is a role play that provides an experiential background for a presentation of the *Johari Window* theory. While the *Johari Window* may sound like something out of oriental philosophy, it is simply a structure for taking a better look at how we see ourselves and use feedback about ourselves in the context of our "self-images." It is a framework for improved self-understanding through interpersonal communication and feedback. The accompanying activity provides an opportunity for self-disclosure and self-learning and serves as a vehicle for learning how to give and receive feedback.

Contents

Trainer Instructions: Contains purpose, details of the set-up, and step-by-step instructions for conducting the role play.

Johari Window Lecturette: Provides format for presenting the theory.*

Feedback Session: Contains directions for conducting this activity.

Bob, Carol, Ted and Alec: Two short role plays to provide an experiential background for the *Johari Window* model.

Johari Window Worksheet: A sheet that provides a simple format for practicing the giving and receiving of feedback to improve the benefits from this activity.

Guidelines for Giving Feedback: Ground rules for giving feedback.

Guidelines for Receiving Feedback: Ground rules for receiving feedback.

* The lecturette is a greatly simplified explanation of this concept. If the facilitator would like to do a more thorough presentation, please refer to *Of Human Interaction* by Joseph Luft, Mayfield Publishing Company, Palo Alto, CA, 1969.

Trainer Instructions

Purpose

This activity is designed to demonstrate the importance of giving and receiving feedback in a relationship. If constructive feedback is a norm for individuals, teams, and the organization as a whole, it is likely that the trust level will be fairly high. When trust is high, relationships are both more productive and more satisfying.

Set-Up

"Bob, Carol, Ted and Alec" may be used with any number of people. "Bob and Carol" is conducted with pairs of people; "Ted and Alec" requires four to five people. Generally, larger groups of twenty-five or more are sub-grouped into smaller groups of five to six.

The activity begins with a discussion by small groups of the "Bob, Carol, Ted and Alec" cases. After more general discussion, pairs are formed to roleplay Bob and Carol. The entire "small group" roleplays Ted and Alec as a meeting between colleagues and their respective bosses.

The role plays are followed by a trainer input on the *Johari Window* theory.

The theory input is followed by practice in giving and receiving feedback within the small groups. A copy of the two role plays and the feedback sheets follows at the end of this chapter.

Steps

1. Tell the total group that you would like to introduce two short cases to focus on certain communication principles. Hand out one copy of the "Bob, Carol, Ted and Alec" case to each person. Allow approximately ten minutes for people to read the cases and make a few notes.

2. After the cases have been studied, ask the small groups to take about fifteen minutes to discuss them. The questions to be answered include: "What is the source of these communication problems?" and "What must be done to put these relationships back on track?" When the small group discussions are concluded, ask for a spokesperson from each group to summarize the group's discussion and recommendations.

3. Groups usually produce superficial recommendations in response to these two situations. Their recommendations do not take into account the difficulty in repairing these relationships. For example, in the Bob and Carol case, people generally say that "Carol should sit down and talk to Bob."

4. As soon as the above suggestion is offered, ask the groups to engage in a few minutes of "reality practice." Ask everyone in the room to form pairs. One person will play the role of Bob and the other will play the role of Carol. This direction will cause a good deal of confusion, laughter, and noise. Before starting, check to see that for every Bob there is a Carol.

5. Ask the role players to spend five to ten minutes preparing for a conversation between Carol and Bob, focusing on Bob's performance and attempting to get his cooperation. Then, begin the role play.

6. After the role play has been in progress for five to six minutes, stop the action and ask everyone to exchange roles. All of the Carols now become Bobs and vice versa. Again, allow the role play to continue for about five minutes.

7. When the participants have had ample opportunity to play both parts, lead the group in a discussion of the case.

   Ask: "What was the purpose of this discussion?" This sounds like a simple question, but the participants often are not clear about what is supposed to come out of this discussion. The answer is that Carol wants Bob to change his performance to meet her standards.

8. Now ask if the Bobs have been persuaded by Carol to change their performance. In most cases, the response will be "No." A few people who did not get into their characters may respond positively, but most will be resistant and unresponsive to Carol's evaluation.

9. Then ask how Carol opened the discussion. Most Carols will describe a logical analysis of Bob's past performance and why he needs to change. These analyses will be perfectly reasonable, but the problem is the relationship itself. Any discussion of the reasonableness of Carol's observations and request must be preceded by a discussion of Bob's and Carol's relationship. This means that the feelings the parties have for each other must be put on the table and opened up for discussion. For example, Carol must discuss Bob's feelings about not getting her job; Bob's feelings about working for someone younger and with less experience; and even how Bob feels about working for a female boss. Unless these issues are discussed, communication cannot grow healthier, even though no resolution to these issues may be possible. The basis of all human relationships is the feelings the parties have for each other. Once these have been dealt with adequately, a rational discussion of Bob's need to change may be held. In the organizational setting we are used to being reasonable and not attending to people's feelings. The issue here is Bob's and Carol's relationship. The basis of all human relationships is feeling(s).

10. When you have debriefed the Bob and Carol exercise, turn next to the Ted and Alec case. One of the issues in Ted and Alec is "who goes first?" Who should take the initiative and apologize to the other person to get the relationship back on track? Trying to answer this usually results in a stalemate. The second

issue usually revolves around whether the vice presidents should handle the matter. Assuming that one of the spokespeople suggests that the vice presidents and their employees should convene a meeting to resolve the problem, suggest another reality practice, this time following a meeting format. The small team should decide who will play Ted, Alec, and the two vice presidents. Remember that one of the vice presidents has more organizational "clout" than the other. Extra participants may be observers.

11 Allow approximately ten minutes for this discussion. Ask a spokesperson to summarize the meeting and what was accomplished. In very few cases will groups report resolving the issue. The vice presidents complicate the problem, even if they try to be scrupulously fair to all concerned. Sometimes Ted and Alec will get into a new argument. The vice presidents will be forced to take sides, sometimes against their own employee. The permutations are numerous, but one thing is clear — resolving personal disagreements is *not* easily done in a group setting. The parties must find a way to talk about their relationship. Any other solution will not be long term.

12. The trainer should now use this opportunity to point out the importance of having a way of looking at communication and interpersonal relationships. That "way" is the *Johari Window*. You may use the following outline of the Johari Theory for your presentation. The lecturette is written from an organizational perspective.

Johari Theory Lecturette

Introduction

1. The *Johari Window* is a model of interpersonal communication: one-to-one communication.

2. "O was some Power the giftie gie us
To see oursels as ithers see us!"

> Robert Burns, Ode to a Louse
> (On Seeing One on a Lady's Bonnet
> at Church), 1786

In Swahili *Johari* means "someone who is brave and strong." In Hindi it refers to someone who knows about jewels. In Arabic *Johari* means "gold," and in ancient Sanskrit it translates as "the god who sees within." But the term *Johari Window* refers not to the precious gems, metals, heroes, or gods, but to a simple and useful idea first developed by *Joseph Luft* and *Harrington Ingham.*

3. Communication is a much overworked word. What we often call "communication problems" might be better referred to as unsound relationships, which in turn cause the communication problems.

4. At the base of sound relationships with others is the mutual sharing of interpersonal data. In the organizational setting we are looking for sharing of organization-related information, as well as personal reactions and feelings about what is occurring in the organization. It means being open; letting people know what you are thinking.

The Model

1. The *Johari Window* is an awareness model — indicating the extent to which you are aware of the impact of your communication style on others, as well as on yourself.

2. When two people come together to communicate, both have information of which they are aware (Known) and can share if they choose. There is also information both possess which they are not consciously aware of (Unknown), but which affects the relationship nonetheless.

3. How we use the interpersonal communication space makes a difference in the quantity and quality of production and satisfaction in the relationship.

4. Like most windows, the *Johari Window* has four sides. In this model the top and bottom of the window refer to our self-perceptions, things we know about ourselves and things we do not know. The sides refer to others' perceptions of us, in terms of things they know about us and things they do not know. Thus, the *Johari Window* has four "panes":

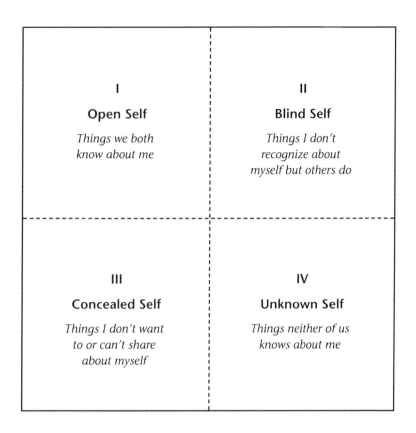

I **Open Self** *Things we both know about me*	**II** **Blind Self** *Things I don't recognize about myself but others do*
III **Concealed Self** *Things I don't want to or can't share about myself*	**IV** **Unknown Self** *Things neither of us knows about me*

The Johari Awareness Model

(1) **Open Self:** things I know about myself that others also know; (2) **Blind Self:** things I do not know about myself but that others can see; (3) **Concealed Self:** things I know about myself that others do not know; and (4) **Unknown Self:** things neither I nor others know about me. The *Johari Window* is a convenient way to categorize our knowledge or perceptions of ourselves. It can be useful by helping us focus on obtaining more knowledge (feedback) from others and helping us work on ways to share more information about ourselves with others.

By directing our information search and our information sharing efforts, the *Johari Window* can help us to develop a more healthy self-image and a more open and self-disclosing interpersonal communication style. The *Johari Window* is a "giftie," as Burns would say, a little gift, but it can prove of great value if used well.

The Four Informational Areas

1. **Area I** — represents information which is mutually shared by both parties.

   a. It is called the **Open Self** — sometimes the public arena to indicate its shared nature.

   b. It is the most important area in the window. Because of its shared nature it produces the highest levels of productivity and satisfaction for both parties.

   c. It means that the ideas, information, data, feelings, and reactions relevant to the business situation are openly and honestly shared with one another.

   d. Some personal data is no doubt shared as well, but it is organizational information and reactions relevant to the organizational setting that we are concerned about here.

2. **Area II** — represents information the other party has but you are unaware of it.

   a. It is called the **Blind Self**. You have a blindspot in your relations with the other party.

   b. Each time you do or say something, you trigger at least one and probably several reactions in the other person.

   c. If you don't specifically ask for that person's reactions to what you are doing, he / she builds a databank of information that would be useful to you. It could help you adjust your behavior toward that person. That information can be used against you if the other party chooses.

   d. Some personal data is no doubt shared as well, but again, it is organizational information and reactions that we are focusing on.

   e. The other party gets frustrated if he / she has no opportunity for input in the relationship. He / she feels undervalued.

   f. We all have some blindspots — we don't know everything that others are thinking or feeling about us.

3. **Area III** — represents the data you have, but have chosen not to share.

   a. It is called the **Concealed Self**.

   b. You can build a protective wall around yourself, but in doing so, you keep yourself cut off from others.

   c. People hold back for a variety of reasons: they are naturally shy; they feel inferior; they don't feel accepted; they want to build a power base by keeping information to themselves.

   d. However, others need this information to operate effectively with you. They need to be able to predict your behavior; to understand you.

   e. The relationship loses its foundation of trust if you are not perceived as being open. Others begin to hold back when they realize there is much about you they don't know.

   f. Everyone has some part of themselves that is concealed; we aren't totally open.

4. **Area IV** — represents information neither party has access to.

   a. It is called the ***Unknown Self***.

   b. We all have hopes, desires, latent talents, things we would like to do or become. If we don't surface, share, and develop these, they are lost to us, the relationship, and the organization as a whole. We pass up the opportunity to realize all that we are capable of.

   c. The Unknown Self houses our keener insights, imagination, and creativity. If we heavily screen what we allow to come through, we become conventional. There is a sameness about our interactions with others.

   d. We all have an Unknown Self. It is only through self-analysis and sharing our inner self with others that we can come to know what our potential might be.

5. **Review** — the Window has four areas:

   a. Area I = ***Open Self*** — data that is shared. It is the most important area because it determines the productivity and satisfaction both parties find in the relationship.

   b. Area II = ***Blind Self*** — information others have about you that you have not tapped into. It makes you vulnerable to them.

   c. Area III = ***Concealed Self*** — information you have kept to yourself for whatever reason. Others lose their trust in you.

   d. Area IV = ***Unknown Self*** — your hidden potential is lost because you have not surfaced and developed it. Your hidden needs cause you to behave in certain ways, however, and that affects the relationship.

6. Once the theory is understood, point out that Carol had a very large blindspot in her relationship with Bob. This was also true of Ted and Alec in their relationship with each other. If their relationships are to improve, then each must find ways of obtaining information from their Blind Self. This means initiating the feedback process from the other party in hopes of improving working relationships.

   Everyone needs feedback on the impact of their behavior if they are to be effective in their relations with others. The Johari model provides a convenient method for practicing the giving and receiving of feedback. Tell the group that you want to provide an opportunity for this practice to occur.

Feedback Session

1. Hand out copies of the "Johari Window Worksheet." Ask the participants to form small groups of three or four, choosing others with whom they would feel comfortable sharing generally unknown information about themselves. Or they could stay with their present groups.

2. When the groups are formed, ask everyone to write three things about themselves in the Open Self pane on the worksheet and two more things about themselves in the Concealed Self pane. Emphasize that the items in the Concealed Self pane should not be "deep dark secrets," but can simply be things that others might not know about them. Allow about ten minutes. Tell them to put their name on the worksheet.

3. Give each participant a copy of "Guidelines for Giving Feedback" and a copy of "Guidelines for Receiving Feedback." Allow ten to fifteen minutes for reading and understanding the Guidelines.

4. Instruct each person to pass his or her "Johari Window Worksheet" to the person on his/her right. Each person then is to write one item on that group member's worksheet, in the Blind Self pane. That item should tell the person owning the worksheet something about him/herself that the writer believes the person does not realize (but that the writer does). The papers are passed again and this is repeated until everyone in the group has written one item in the Blind Self pane of every other person's Johari Window. Emphasize that in doing this, participants are to practice the skills of giving effective feedback. That is, the feedback statements should be descriptive (not interpretive), specific (not general), nonevaluative, timely (not delayed), requested (not imposed), deal with easy-to-control behavior (not habitual), and be designed to help (not hurt).

5. When the individuals get back their own "Johari Window Worksheets," they should read what the others in their group have written. Each person should then have an opportunity to ask questions about the Blind Self items the others have written to him or her. Allow five to ten minutes for small group discussion. Remind them to follow the "Guidelines for Giving Feedback."

6. Call everyone back into a single large group for a discussion of what they have learned about themselves. Some relevant questions include:
   a. What did you learn about yourself that you did not already know?
   b. Was it difficult to share some "hidden" aspects of yourself?
   c. How hard was it to give Blind Self feedback that met the seven guidelines?
   d. Did the feedback you received really get through your "filters"?

7. Add any other closing comments you feel are helpful or necessary.

Bob, Carol, Ted and Alec

Two Cases of Communication Breakdown

Directions: With your team, diagnose each situation and develop a recommended course of action.

Case I — Bob and Carol

Carol, a recently appointed food and beverage manager in a mid-size hotel, is concerned about her working relationship with Bob, a long service "professional" restaurant manager. Carol is twenty-nine years old and was recruited from another hotel. She has a reputation in this industry for being a strongly aggressive, high-powered manager. This is her first assignment at this level. She is, of course, anxious that it be a successful one. She has five restaurant managers reporting to her, most of them young and inexperienced, but all showing promise during the previous season.

Bob has twenty-seven years of experience, five within the company. He is fifty-two years old, in good health, and not thinking of retirement or other career moves. His work has been rated satisfactory by his previous food and beverage manager. Although he has a fairly well-developed restaurant business, there are scheduling problems, food supplier problems, kitchen problems, and other indications of deteriorating quality and service. Carol has evaluated Bob's current performance as "just satisfactory" and would like to help him improve.

Carol has had several conversations with Bob about his business. These conversations have consisted mainly of Carol rapidly listing her observations and recommendations and Bob listening, saying little, but looking somewhat sullen. Carol suspects that Bob may think that she is too young for the job. Other restaurant managers have confided to her that Bob applied for her job before she arrived and was "very disappointed" when he was turned down. It has also been rumored that Bob has some "friends" in high positions in the company.

Case II — Ted and Alec

Ted is an experienced systems manager in Compudata's Harrisburg office. He is responsible for a staff and other resources that cost Compudata nearly a half million dollars per year. His performance in his current role has been above average for the last two years. Alec is the installation manager for the Corporate Systems Department. He, too, is experienced in his job and his department has been performing better than anticipated when he first took his position two years ago. Both men are regarded by senior corporate management as strong and promotable. Both men are competitive, ego-centered individuals. Each has strong opinions, reinforced by long-term career success.

About a week ago, Alec visited the Harrisburg office with several of his staff members. Without talking to Ted beforehand, Alec and his staff held informal meetings with several of Ted's employees to discuss current systems development and applications work taking place in Harrisburg. During these meetings he suggested a rearrangement of priorities within the Harrisburg systems unit. In Alec's opinion, several of the projects on which emphasis was being placed in Harrisburg were not priority issues and this was resulting in slowing down several major projects both in Harrisburg and at the corporate level. (Ted's unit has had severe difficulties in getting certain projects brought to conclusion at the regional level in comparison to other Compudata facilities.) The assistant manager of the Harrisburg systems staff, who in turn reports to Ted, did not intervene as these meetings took place and was perceived by the Harrisburg systems staff as concurring with Alec's recommendations.

Ted and the production manager for Harrisburg happened to pass by the Systems Department. After talking with a few systems employees, they realized what Alec was doing and told him to discontinue further meetings. A heated argument ensued, resulting in Alec and his staff being asked to leave the Harrisburg facility.

Both men immediately brought the situation to the attention of their respective vice presidents. Because the balance of "political" power appears to favor the corporate systems function, this conflict may be resolved in favor of Alec.

Johari Window Worksheet

Name _____

Open Self	Blind Self
1. _____ _____ _____ _____ 2. _____ _____ _____ _____ 3. _____ _____ _____ _____	1. _____ _____ _____ 2. _____ _____ 3. _____ _____ 4. _____ _____ _____
Concealed Self 1. _____ _____ _____ _____ 2. _____ _____ _____ _____	**Unknown Self**

Guidelines For Receiving Feedback

1. *Understand What Was Said*

   Remain silent. Actively listen. Look for nonverbal as well as verbal feedback. Ask for clarification or amplification, if desired, when the sender is finished.

   "Could you tell me a little more about your reaction to that?"

   Paraphrase your understanding of the sender's feedback.

   "In other words, you thought I wasn't interested in the group discussion because I didn't readily volunteer my thoughts?"

2. *Be Open Rather than Defensive*

   Approach feedback with an "I want to learn about myself" attitude. Feedback represents the other person's experience. It is neither right nor wrong.

   Avoid explaining your behavior. Don't give causes, reasons, or excuses.

   Try to see the feedback from the other person's point of view.

3. *Separate Yourself from Your Behavior*

   Try to maintain a sense of your personal worth and view the feedback as a description of your behavior as it affects another person. As a person, you are OK. If your behavior creates a problem for others, you can choose whether or not to change that behavior.

4. *Check the "Fit"*

   Try to obtain feedback on the same behavior from several people. Then check to see if it "fits." Does it make sense; does it agree with what you know about yourself; does it agree with what others have said; is it practical; etc.?

   If it "fits," then you can decide whether or not you want to change or modify the behavior. If it doesn't "fit," you can reject it.

Guidelines For Giving Feedback

1. *Description vs. Interpretation of Behavior*

   Describe how the behavior made you feel rather than interpreting the other person's behavior. Commenting on someone's motive or intention puts them on the defensive.

   > "When you quickly dismissed my ideas, I felt embarrassed and put down." (Descriptive)

   > "You must not like me. You seemed so hostile toward me during the group discussion this morning." (Interpretation)

2. *Specific vs. General Feedback*

   Comments such as, "You are judgmental" or "You are a supportive person" do not describe specific behavior. (General)

   > "When you defended me at lunch today, I felt grateful to you." (Specific)

3. *Nonevaluative vs. Evaluative Feedback*

   Nonevaluative feedback describes your feelings about the *behavior* and how the behavior affects you. Evaluative feedback passes judgment on the other person and is difficult to respond to because it offends that person's feelings of self-worth.

   > "You tend to be insensitive to the feelings and needs of others." (Evaluative)

   > "I felt embarrassed when you discounted my suggestions during the last group discussion. (Nonevaluative)

4. *Immediate vs. Delayed Timing*

   The most effective feedback is given immediately following the behavior and acts as a mirror on that behavior.

   If giving feedback has been established as a norm, then periodic feedback sessions can be planned.

5. *Requested vs. Imposed Feedback*

   Feedback which has been requested is usually more helpful to the sender because he/she is prepared for it.

   If a norm for giving feedback exists, spontaneous feedback can be helpful and fills the requirement of immediacy.

6. *Easy-to-Control vs. Difficult-to-Control Behavior*

    Feedback on habitual behavior can be frustrating and usually doesn't help the situation. You may have to directly ask if the person thinks that the behavior can be modified.

    "I find it hard to work on projects with you because you smoke so heavily. Do you think you could cut back on it?"

7. *Motivation to Help vs. Motivation to Hurt*

    Feedback given in anger is often useless because it puts the receiver in a defensive position to protect his/her self-image.

    The best approach is to deal with the anger directly. Acknowledge your angry feelings without placing any responsibility for those feelings on the other person.

    "I am feeling angry about your criticism of my department during the meeting yesterday. Could we get together sometime today and talk about it?"

Structured Activity   13

Modern Manufacturing, Inc.

Summary

This case study is called an "in-basket exercise. All of the materials to be worked with take the form of the contents of incoming mail and telephone calls. The participants will work through the problem independently. When they have finished, they will discuss their answers in a small group and arrive at group decisions. A spokesperson from each group will report the decisions and rationales to the total group.

Because of the more complex nature of this activity, a detailed Trainer Guide has been prepared. The in-basket worksheets for the participants are in the Participant Kit.

Contents

Modern Manufacturing, Inc.
Trainer Guide

General Information

Effective communication achieves desired results. This end is best served when the communicator takes the time to: clearly identify the objective, carefully select the audience, choose a method that best suits the situation, and form the message to get results.

This exercise is not a test of skill in forming the message. In most organizations communications go awry as a result of failure in strategy. This case study focuses on the total process of communication strategy. Even in the most obvious situation one must take the time to plan.

The "Modern Manufacturing" exercise provides organizational communication situations. As members of the organization, the participants will be called upon to respond to these situations with concern for optimum organizational and personal outcomes.

This exercise deals with communication strategy. It does not attempt to teach communication skills. It addresses the process steps that should precede and are critical to the act of communicating.

Effective communication strategy includes a structured approach to the situation. The four strategic steps are:

1. *Establish Communication Objectives.* Clear communication that does the job seldom grows out of a message, oral or written, if the communicator has not identified a desired result. Think about the situation before you start. What is it that you want to have happen?

2. *Select the Audience and Respect the Organization Structure.* The objective is the key to selecting the primary audience. Who must do something or decide that it should be done in order to achieve your desired result? Who, because of their positions in the hierarchy, deserve to know? These decisions should be made with respect for the channels of authority and responsibility yet with a practical understanding of how the organization works.

3. *Determine the Best Method.* The most available methods of communication are oral, either by telephone or face-to-face, and written. The latter method has various levels of formality. The determining factors are usually the nature of the message, the size of the audience, and the relationship between you and the primary audience.

4. *State the Purpose of Your Communication Early.* If convincing is necessary, support your point of view with reasons that have meaning or value to the audience. If you desire action, call for it at the end. Keep it short and simple.

The Process

This case study provides the participants with situations calling for decisions in communication strategy. They will practice the process of determining: the objective, the audience, the method, and the message. The participants will also face problems and potential problems generated by the communication practices of others in the organization. Their success in this exercise can be measured in part by how they deal with these practices and whether or not the action taken will improve communication in the future.

This "in-basket" is both an individual and a group exercise. The individual participants complete the exercise and then meet in groups of two to five people. The mission of the sub-groups will be to agree on appropriate action, through consensus, for each of the in-basket items assigned.

When the sub-groups report back to the total group, the trainer and participants should examine each sub-group's decision. It should be tested for its objective(s) and appropriateness of audience, method, and message. If an in-basket item involves an organizational process violation, test the sub-group's decision for how well it dealt with that violation and whether or not it will cause future communication to improve.

Learning Objectives

1. To identify situations requiring communication.

2. To understand the need to:
   • identify the communication objectives.
   • determine the appropriate audience.
   • select the optimum method of transmittal.
   • utilize a structure, style, and length appropriate to the objective.

3. To identify and deal with the organization structure and how it affects the communication process.

Case Information

1. *Type* — In-basket case study

2. *Time* — approximately 2-1/2 hours

3. *Group Size* — This case study can be used with almost any number of participants.
   With seven or fewer participants:
   a. Participants do the in-basket as individuals only.
   b. The trainer asks each of the participants to report on his/her solutions to two or more of the in-basket items. Divide the exercises as evenly as possible among the participants.

With eight or more participants:

a. Participants do the in-basket individually.

b. Divide participants into 3–5 sub-groups of three or more participants.

c. Divide the in-basket items as evenly as possible among the sub-groups.

d. Have the sub-groups arrive at consensus solutions to the assigned items.

e. Ask a spokesperson for each of the sub-groups to report the group's solutions to the total group.

4. *Materials*

Participants: Background/Instructions
Organization Diagram
One set of fourteen in-basket items
Fourteen Analysis Forms
Pencil and paper

Trainer: Trainer Guide
In-basket Index
Twenty Analysis Forms
Flip chart or chalkboard

Setting and Preparation

1. Study the Trainer Guide and complete the in-basket exercise prior to the training session.

2. The meeting room need only be large enough to accommodate the group and instructor, set up in classroom style.

3. Be prepared to divide the participants into sub-groups. You will know the number of participants so plan ahead. Decide the number of sub-groups, the number in each, and how the assignments will be made.

4. Put pencil and paper at each participant's place. The in-basket kit, which you will have reproduced, should be distributed later.

Conducting the Session

1. Introduce yourself and have the participants introduce themselves. (This may be unnecessary with a familiar group.)

2. Introduce the exercise and the subject of communication by summarizing the General Information section at the beginning of this Guide.)

3. Explain the in-basket case study process. (See the Purpose section at the beginning of this activity.)

4. Distribute the participants' material.

5. Have the participants read the Background/Instructions sheet and start the individual exercise. (You may want to use the participant's work time for your own review of the in-basket items and the issues for discussion.)

6. After about one hour, you will find some participants on item #8 or #9 while others are on #12 or #13 and nearly finished. You want them to finish at about the same time.

STOP THE WORK

Make the following announcement: "You have just received a call requiring you to go out of town. To catch your plane, you must be finished with your work so you can leave the office in twenty minutes."

7. Twenty minutes later, stop the work. Most of the participants will have finished.

8. Have the participants form sub-groups of three to five people. When working with *fewer* than eight participants, assign items to the individual participants and go directly to step 12.

9. Assign the in-basket items, divided as evenly as possible between the sub-groups.

10. Give each group an Analysis Form for each item assigned.

11. Instruct the sub-groups to:

   a. discuss each assigned item.

   b. reach a consensus agreement on objective, audience, method, and message.

   c. complete the Analysis Forms.

   d. assign one member of the sub-group to report to the total group.

12. Have each sub-group report back on assigned in-basket items. Call for the reports in order, one through fourteen.

13. After each item is reported, ask for individual comments and observations from members of the other sub-groups. You should find some disagreement on most items. This, and the ensuing discussion, should be encouraged.

14. Use the discussion to ensure that the critical issues of each in-basket item have been addressed.

15. When the last item has been discussed, ask for any general discussion or comment. You may find some participants frustrated by the lack of case information. This can be handled best by noting that there was enough information to deal with the principles involved and to practice the communication process, even though details might have been lacking in some cases.

Closing

Reinforce the need to:

1. establish communications objectives

2. select the audience and respect the organization structure

3. determine the best method

4. create content that does the job.

Guide to Managing the Discussion

General

The issues identified and the recommended communication action are those of the author. They are drawn from communication theory, organizational protocol, and experience.

Participants will not always arrive at the same issue nor will they always agree on appropriate action. This will vary by personal differences, experiences, and exposure to different corporate cultures.

These individual conclusions should not be characterized as wrong. They should be used as springboards for discussion. Learning is more likely to grow out of open discussion than a citation by the trainer that "this is the *correct* response." Compare different views with the author's recommendations and ask for discussion around the differences. A list of discussion questions for each in-basket is at the end of this section.

Issues and Recommendations

C-1 When your boss wants to discuss a report, written by your employee, you would probably make a date for the review. When your boss has discussed the report with his boss, another dimension has been added. A four-step chain of communication from the VP and Chief Engineer to your employee, who authored the report, has great potential for failure. While the VP's response will probably get through, the spirit of his reaction is at risk. Combining links in the chain will reduce this risk.

> *Objective*: To improve the communication process by including Linda Court in the review session.
>
> *Audience*: Joe Sargeant
>
> *Method*: 1st choice — Face to face; 2nd choice — By phone (determined by circumstances).
>
> *Message*: An inquiry as to the nature of the review and the appropriateness of including Linda Court.

C-2 When your boss' boss wants to see you, you will probably show up. The request, however, concerns a subject under review by you and your boss. You have an obligation to your boss to keep him informed. You have an obligation to yourself to know as much as you can when you meet with the VP of Engineering.

> *Objective*: To keep your boss informed and to find out what issues surfaced when he and George Stanley reviewed Linda Court's report.
>
> *Audience*: Joe Sargeant

Method: 1st choice — Face to face; 2nd choice — By phone (determined by available time).

Message: George Stanley wants to see me about re-tooling. What was the outcome of your discussion with him?

Note: You are now ready to make an appointment with George.

C-3   Coaching employees is one of the prime responsibilities of a department head. Project results and the professional growth of the employees depend on it. Hal Late is clearly seeking your help.

It is not uncommon for project engineers and other professionals to have technical responsibility without administrative authority over others. They may not be comfortable in this pseudo-supervisory role. Hal Late may or may not be trying some upward delegation. In either case, avoid the temptation to take over.

Objective: To prepare Hal Late to deal directly and effectively with Rieter and the discrepancies in his recommendations.

Audience: Hal Late

Method: Face to face (personal touch is important here).

Message: After confirming the shortcomings of the report, recommend that Hal explore his concerns with Rieter. What do you expect the line #2 impact to be? How did you evaluate the structural requirement? Recommend in summary that all facets of the project need consideration.

C-4   You realize that the line #3 proposal may impact line #2 and you are having something done about it. Your boss deserves to know about it. Problems between Rieter and manufacturing is news. This calls for more information.

When peer department heads do not communicate directly, unnecessary involvement of others increases and issues tend to get inflated.

A. *Objective*:   Inform the boss that work is in progress on line #3's impact on line #2.

Audience: Joe Sargeant; Secondary — Dan Foss

Method: Memo (some things should be put "on the record").

Message: Thanks — we know about it and are working on it.

Note: When you have learned more about Industrial Engineering's concerns and about Rieter vs. manufacturing, respond to Sargeant's questions about Industrial Engineering's involvement. Find out who originated the idea of an IE takeover.

B. *Objective*:   Get facts about the relationships between Rieter and engineering.

Audience: Hal Late

Method: Face to face

Message: What are the problems, if any? If needed, pursue with Rieter and manufacturing.

C. *Objective*: To get technical assistance from Industrial Engineering and open communication channels with Dan Foss. You would prefer that he handle problems involving your department directly with you.

Audience: Dan Foss

Method: Face to face (delicate situations tend to require this).

Message: We know about the problems with line #2 and could use your help. Call me directly when you see any problems in the future. (The wording will depend on your personal relationship.)

Note: The IE takeover of the project may also be a subject for discussion depending on who originated the idea.

C-5 When a top-level executive makes a request, it is usually honored. The obligation here is to respond to your employee's concern for cost and need. If he can make a good enough case for his position, those points should be made known to George Stanley. Absent a good case, Hal Late should understand the reality of the situation.

Objective: Test Hal Late's opinion that the changes are "expensive and unnecessary."

Audience: Hal Late

Method: Face to face (settle it now) or a note on the memo (let Hal think over his position).

Message: What are the costs and what is George Stanley seeking to achieve with the changes?

C-6 When a boss bypasses a department head by dealing with a member of the department on a continuing basis, the department head may resent being excluded. In this case, it appears that neither Sargeant nor Black have kept Tom Hays informed. Hays may be looking for council or just a friendly ear. In either case, you stand some risk of being hooked.

Objective: To be of reasonable help or support to an associate, keeping in mind that you also report to Sargeant.

Audience: Tom Hays

Method: Face to face (over lunch).

Message: You may just want to listen. It might help to find out why Hays is not holding project review sessions with Bart Black.

C-7 Cross-functional assignments of several months or more are usually good for the organization and a valuable developmental experience for the employee. It is important, however, to establish the ground rules clearly before making the move. These rules should set forth responsibility for: time sheets and other administrative approvals, performance evaluation, merit salary review, and manpower and expense obligations. Your boss has asked you to "work this out."

Objective: To gain Hughes' agreement on administrative issues.

Audience: Carter Hughes

Method: Face to face (you will probably want the conclusions in writing, but there is a better chance of reaching an agreement if the parties meet in person).

Message: I am open and flexible as long as we establish the ground rules clearly. Let's discuss it issue by issue.

C-8 Mentoring (helping the development of a junior member of the organization) sometimes crosses organizational lines. When this happens, an element of risk is introduced. You are apparently caught in a bind between Tom Hays and his employee. Hays has compounded the problem by involving your boss. Sargeant wants to "discuss this soon." So do you.

Objective: To reach your boss as soon as possible to defuse the situation and explore the problems of the relationships involved.

Audience: Joe Sargeant

Method: Face to face (this situation may call for the kind of leveling unsuited to written communication).

Message: Harry Johnson has found it helpful, perhaps necessary, to seek information and guidance from you. Why? If there is a broader problem here, help your boss discover and address it.

C-9 You have just received additional information relative to Tom Hays' complaint regarding your relationship with Harry Johnson. What you have heard, however, is from Harry's perspective.

Objective: Harry thinks he can work it out by himself. You probably should let him. The input gained from the phone call may be helpful when you talk with your boss.

C-10 When input is not sought in a timely fashion, a decision is apt to be made without input from all parties involved. Unfortunately, there are also times when input is sought for the sole purpose of generating a feeling of ownership. The outcomes in these instances are foregone conclusions.

We do not know which was the case here. It is apparent, though, that you have an opportunity to be miffed at wasting your time with an analysis that was requested but never considered. Don't! Remember, you are seeking the best outcome for both you and the organization.

Objective: 1. To reiterate your concerns.

2. To let your boss know that you would have felt better about the situation had your comments been considered.

3. To assure him that your group stands ready to help.

Audience: Joe Sargeant

Method: Objectives 1 and 3 — Memo. Objective 2 — Face to face (when the right occasion presents itself).

Message: Objectives 1 and 3 — List concerns with an analysis of how they can be overcome. Objective 2 — Level with the boss. "I felt that. . . ."

C-11 When you want help from a peer manager, you usually can do quite well directly. When the request is for significant help from a manager at the next higher level, it is time to use your boss' clout. This was not done and you are back to square one. In fact, you may have lost ground. The second time around is often more difficult.

It is time to work this out with your boss. Better late than never.

Objective: To gain support and get action to cover Garrett's project responsibility while he is out.

Audience: Joe Sargeant

Method: Memo (you want to build a case and give him time to think about it).

Message: Essentially what you told Bob Moore but supplemented by measures of work load, staffing, and an assessment of consequences if the problem is not solved. Your boss also needs to know about your initial attempt. Enclose a copy of the Bob Moore memo.

C-12 You have some bad news to pass along to members of your department. It is not earth shattering, but it will be better received if you can tell them why the change is being made and what the approximate cost differential will be.

A. *Objective*: To learn more about the change.

   Audience: A knowledgeable member of the personnel department

   Method: Phone call (you will probably learn more this way).

   Message: Why the change, and what percent of premium have we been saving.

B. *Objective*: To inform department members.

   Audience: The department

   Method: Staff meeting (this allows instant venting of any negative feelings which usually helps).

   Message: The change, the reasons, the impact.

C-13 "Doing it yourself" is often the handiest and easiest route to take. It can also be wrong.

You appear to have two choices. Do it yourself or refer the call to Linda Court. Handling it yourself would be faster, save time for one of your busy staff members, and impress the sub-contractor's representative. On the other hand, it is Linda's project. The call should have come to her. Future calls should come to her. It would be worthwhile to bolster her relationship with the sub-contractor's representative by having her handle it.

Objective: Transfer the call.

Audience: Linda Court

Method: Phone transfer

Message: This call is in regard to your re-tooling project.

Note: If you opt to handle this yourself, let Linda know.

C-14 Linda needs help in getting action from another department. She also needs to maintain her relationship with the buyer on the project. A call from you to Janet Cyr would probably settle the matter. It might also generate ill feelings between Bob Jones and Linda. This project is just getting started and cooperation down the line is important. A call to Jones directly might do the trick, but carries the same risk as the call to his boss. How about coaching Linda Court on the skills of getting cooperation from members of other departments?

Objective: Help Linda Court to get needed action from purchasing with intervention by you as a last resort.

Audience: Linda Court

Method: Face to face

Message: Direct a coaching conference toward ways in which Linda can cooperation outside the department. This could include an offer of assistance to Jones; a discussion of alternative ways of getting the information; reducing the request to essential data, if possible; and asking Bob Jones for his suggestions.

Note: If you go this route and it does not work, make your call.

In-Basket Questions for Discussion

C-1   Is this a routine review?

C-2   Is an organizational skip protocol?
How do you handle this?
Do you address the propriety of the skip?
Do you involve Sargeant?

C-3   Why go to the boss? Why not coach?
Do you address the engineering report or who is responsible for what?

C-4   Sargeant: What are the problems reported between Rieter and manufacturing?
Do you support Foss, Sargeant, manufacturing, or Rieter?
Where does Late fit in?
Is Rieter the problem?

C-5   What are the cross-functional complications?
Is Hal right? Are the changes "unnecessary"?
Does Sargeant know about this?
What is the best communication route?
Who needs to agree?
Should Simonds have touched base with Late and Grief?

C-6   Is this your problem?
How involved should you get?
What communication channels are a problem?

C-7   Who should have the responsibility for supervision-administration?

C-8   Is this your problem or Sargeant's?
What is the probable heart of the problem?
How should it be handled?

C-9   Is any action called for here? (Refer to C-8.)

C-10   Why ask for comments if the decision is made?
Is there a need to level with Sargeant?
Should you cooperate with the move?

C-11   Should Sargeant have been involved?
Can you convince Moore?
Would Sargeant help?
Should Stanley be involved?
How about a temporary assignment of Bill Good?

C-12   How do you tell your department?
Do you need to know more?
What is your objective?

C-13   Do you handle this? How?

C-14   Whom do you contact?
Do you throw it back to Court?
Do you get help from higher up in your organization?

Participant Kit

Contents

Modern Manufacturing, Inc.

Background Information

Assume that you are Bob Grief, manager of plant engineering of Modern Manufacturing, Inc. Your staff is shown on the partial organization chart on the next page. (You may wish to keep the chart before you as you go through the exercise.) You report to Joe Sargeant, Director of Mechanical Engineering. He is shown on the chart along with other functional department heads. You are located in the corporate headquarters in Midville, Massachusetts. The company has plants in Massachusetts and New Hampshire.

This exercise emphasizes administrative aspects of the management job, especially as they pertain to communication. Omitted are unimportant technical, financial, and administrative details. This is intentional; it makes it easier to assume the role of Bob Grief and address the issues around which the case study was designed.

The trainer will give you additional information as the exercise progresses.

Instructions

You have been supplied with enough work sheets to use one Analysis Form per basket item. These forms are designed to help organize the communication process. They are not, in themselves, a process. Feel free to improvise.

When you have finished, the trainer will assign you to a sub-group. The sub-group's mission will be to agree, through consensus, and report back to the main group the appropriate action on each of the in-basket items assigned.

You should proceed now with the in-basket exercise.

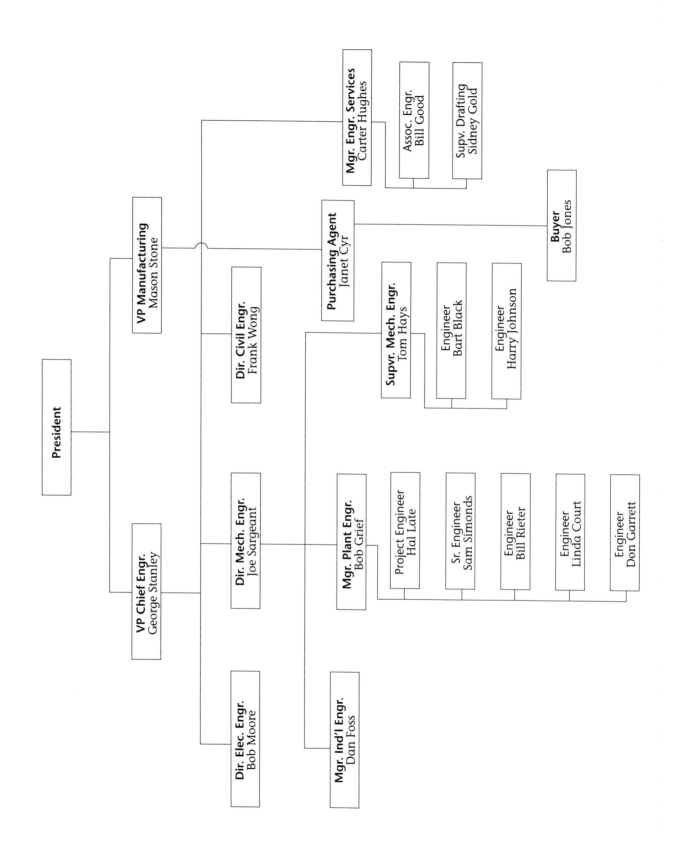

Memorandum C-1

TO: Bob Grief

FROM: Joe Sargeant

George and I have read Linda Court's report on re-tooling for next year's line.

I would like to review it with you.

Joe

Bob —

Please see me

about re-tooling

for next year.

George

Memorandum C-3

TO: Bob Grief

FROM: Hal Late

Bill Rieter has submitted his report to me on line #3 recommending an expenditure of over $200,000.

He has completely missed several important considerations including the impact on line #2 and the possible need for structural foundation work.

Any thoughts on handling this?

Memorandum C-4

TO: Bob Grief

FROM: Joe Sargeant

Dan Foss understands that the proposal on line #3 may affect the output on line #2. Line #2 is already a problem.

Confidentially, I have heard there are some problems between Rieter, who worked on the proposal, and manufacturing. Is this job more suited to the Industrial Engineering group? Foss thinks his staff should be more involved.

Memorandum C-5

Bob –
I think both of
these changes are
expensive and
unnecessary.
Hal

TO: Carter Hughes

FROM: Sam Simonds

    George Stanley has asked me to add window replacements and fence relocation to the beautification project at the Adamsville plant.

    I will need the property plan and a front elevation drawing of the building.

cc: H. Late

C-6

You have just received a phone call from Tom Hays. He wanted to have lunch with you and seek your advice on an organizational problem. Joe Sargeant has been dealing directly with Bart Black on the plans for the new plant in New Hampshire. This has been going on for six months and Tom has reached the point where he has no idea how the project is progressing.

You think he may be looking for ideas on how to handle the situation.

Memorandum C-7

TO: Joe Sargeant

FROM: Carter Hughes

BOB — PLEASE OUTLINE YOUR THOUGHTS AND WORK THIS OUT WITH HUGHES.

Joe

As agreed to at last week's meeting with George Stanley, I have arranged to release Bill Good to Grief's plant engineering group. The initial assignment will be full-time for six months followed by six months at half-time. This will be a good developmental experience for Bill while helping plant engineering out of a tight spot.

I will retain Good on my table of organization, but he will be assigned to Bob Grief.

We should agree on responsibility for supervision, administration, etc.

Memorandum C-8

TO: Bob Grief

FROM: Joe Sargeant

___

Tom Hays' recent performance review of Harry Johnson uncovered an organizational problem involving you. Harry was criticized for going directly to you for technical information. Tom was obviously sensitive to this but what really has him upset are those occasions when Harry has gone to you for administrative information.

That group does not report to you. Tom has a point. Can we discuss this soon?

C-9

You have just received a phone call from Harry Johnson. He seemed very upset about his performance review. Hays had criticized him for going to you for technical and administrative information.

Harry explained to you that he had a hard time dealing with Tom Hays. Tom, it seems, passes a minimum of both technical and administrative information along to his staff and is very uncomfortable when they query him.

When you asked if there was anything he wanted you to do, Harry said, "No, I guess I can work it out myself, but thanks for letting me get it off my chest."

Memorandum C-10

TO: Joe Sargeant

FROM: Bob Grief

BOB—
THANKS FOR YOUR INPUT BUT
THE DECISION HAS ALREADY
BEEN MADE. WE WILL BE
LOOKING FOR A LOT OF HE[L]
FROM YOUR GROUP ON
THE MOVE.
Joe

I have attached my comments to your copy of the proposal to move the automotive lines out of state. I know we can use the space here, but I have some serious reservations about breaking up the production lines. This is all detailed in my comments.

Memorandum C-11

TO: Bob Moore

FROM: Bob Grief

Bob Sorry but we just can't handle it BM

Don Garrett has been the project leader on the "missile" job for the past three months. As you may know, he has been out sick for the past month, and it looks like two more months.

As much of this work is in your electrical group, could you assign someone to project responsibility until Don returns?

Memorandum C-12   Bob —

FOR YOUR INFO

Joe

TO: Functional Vice Presidents

FROM: Norman Conway, Vice President Personnel

Effective the first of next year the group automobile insurance will no longer be available.

Employees insured under the plan should arrange for individual coverage between now and the time that their current policy runs out.

C-13

You have just received a telephone call from Industrial Technologies, a subcontractor on the re-tooling project for next year's line. Their customer representative wants to check the materials requirements.

Linda Court has been handling this project, but a copy of the specifications happens to be right on the top of your desk. It would take less than five minutes to check the materials yourself.

Memorandum C-14

TO: Bob Grief

FROM: Linda Court

I am having difficulty getting delivery dates and pricing from purchasing for the re-tooling project. Bob Jones, the buyer on the project, claims they are too busy, but I need the numbers for next week's report meeting.

Would you see what you could do?

Analysis Form

Item No. _____

I. Overall Objective

_____

_____

II. Communication Audience

Must Inform	Should Inform	Nice to Inform
A _____	D _____	G _____
B _____	E _____	H _____
C _____	F _____	I _____

III. Communication Method (enter appropriate letter from II above)

Formal Report	_____	Staff Meeting	_____
Memo	_____	Face-to-Face	_____
Informal Note	_____	Phone Call	_____
Personal Letter	_____	Mention When Convenient	_____
Bulletin Board	_____	No Communication	_____

IV. Message (content or outline)

_____

_____

_____

V. Comments

_____

_____

_____

Contributor Biographies

Bradford Greason brings over twenty-five years of experience in program development and administration to the human resources arena. As Training Manager, Director of Labor Relations, and Director of Personnel Resources for the New England Electric System companies, he has been manager, instructor, negotiator, and internal consultant.

Bradford holds a B.S. in Mechanical Engineering from Norwich University and is a registered professional engineer in the Commonwealth of Massachusetts. He is currently serving on the Personnel Committee of the New England Science Center and is a member of the Board of Fellows of Norwich University.

Rollin Glaser is president of Organization Design and Development, Inc. In addition to his administrative responsibilities, he is a consultant, trainer, and writer. His previous experience includes being a vice president of organization planning and development for several firms. Rollin holds a B.S. from Northwestern University; an M.Ed. from Northeastern University; has done doctoral work in adult education at Boston University; and is completing his doctorate in adult education at Columbia University. Rollin is the author of *Personnel Management for Retailers* (Lebhar-Friedman, 1977) and co-author of *The Management of Training* (Addison-Wesley, 1970) and *Managing by Design* (Addison-Wesley, 1981).